"Darla Weaver invites readers into her winsome and rural Old Order Mennonite life as she spends each Tuesday with extended family in *Gathering of Sisters*. As the year unspools, Weaver shares stories of seasonal activities, family anecdotes, and a few timely recipes. Rich in reminders to slow down and savor the blessings and moments of the ordinary, this book and its impact will linger long after the last page is turned."
—*Suzanne Woods Fisher, bestselling author of* Amish Peace: Simple Wisdom for a Complicated World

"Darla Weaver opens up her heart and life in this wonderful book that throbs with joy, laughter, and love on every page. Story after story takes us inside her fascinating world on a backroad to heaven."
—*Donald B. Kraybill, author of* Simply Amish

"In *Gathering of Sisters*, Darla Weaver has turned the ordinary into something special. Her Tuesday get-togethers with her mother, sisters, nieces, and nephews are full of picnics, hearty meals, plants, and planning. Reading this delightful collection of Tuesday vignettes, we share in wedding stories and s'mores, stamp art, children's auctioneering, cooking, new babies, and bike rides in all weather. This is a charming read!"
—*Karen M. Johnson-Weiner, professor of anthropology emerita at SUNY Potsdam, studying and writing about Old Order culture for thirty-five years*

"*Gathering of Sisters* is all about maintaining strong family bonds. In this fast-paced world we're living in, the author's family takes time to meet with extended family on a weekly basis, thus passing on the importance of family gatherings to the next generation. The children of these sisters have a book full of precious memories: three generations sharing work, play, meals, smiles, and tears, undoubtedly strengthened by their common faith."

—*Linda Maendel, author of* Hutterite Diaries: Wisdom from My Prairie Community

"Darla Weaver's book is so beautifully written, I felt like I was being welcomed into that warm and loving Old Order Mennonite family, and becoming part of the gathering of sisters."

—*Serena B. Miller of Sugarcreek, Ohio, is the multi-award-winning author of* Love's Journey

GATHERING
of
SISTERS

Herald Press
PO Box 866, Harrisonburg, Virginia 22803
www.HeraldPress.com

Library of Congress Cataloging-in-Publication Data
Names: Weaver, Darla, author.
Title: Gathering of sisters : a year with my old order Mennonite family /
  Darla Weaver.
Description: Harrisonburg : Herald Press, 2018. | Series: Plainspoken :
  real-life stories of Amish and Mennonites
Identifiers: LCCN 2018016629 | ISBN 9781513803371 (pbk. : alk. paper)
Subjects: LCSH: Weaver, Darla. | Weaver, Darla--Family. | Old Order
  Mennonites--Biography. | Mennonite women--Religious life.
Classification: LCC BX8141 .W38 2018 | DDC 289.7092/52 [B] --dc23 LC
  record available at https://lccn.loc.gov/2018016629

Unless otherwise noted, Scripture text is quoted from *The Holy Bible, King James Version*.

GATHERING OF SISTERS
© 2018 by Herald Press, Harrisonburg, Virginia 22803. 800-245-7894.
All rights reserved.
Library of Congress Control Number: 2018016629
International Standard Book Number: 978-1-5138-0337-1 (paperback);
978-1-5138-0339-5 (ebook)
Printed in United States of America
Cover and interior design by Merrill Miller
Cover photo by Bill Coleman

22 21 20 19 18   10 9 8 7 6 5 4 3 2 1

GATHERING
of
SISTERS

A Year with My Old Order Mennonite Family

DARLA WEAVER

HERALD
P R E S S

Harrisonburg, Virginia

This book is a tribute of gratitude to my parents,
Richard and Marie Wenger,
better known as Dad and Mom to the nine of us.

You taught us to:
Love God
Serve him gladly
Cherish family
Count our blessings
Work hard
Smell the flowers
Appreciate life's little things
and
Keep our promises

CONTENTS

INTRODUCTION TO

PL△INSPOKEN
Real-life stories of Amish and Mennonites

AMISH NOVELS, Amish tourist sites, and television shows offer second- or third-hand accounts of Amish, Mennonite, and Hutterite life. Some of these messages are sensitive and accurate. Some are not. Many are flat-out wrong.

Now readers can listen directly to the voices of these Anabaptists themselves through Plainspoken. In the books in this series, readers get to hear Amish, Mennonite, and Hutterite writers talk about the texture of their daily lives: how they spend their time, what they value, what makes them laugh, and how they summon strength from their Christian faith and community.

Plain Anabaptists are publishing their writing more than ever before. But this literature is read mostly by other Amish, Mennonites, and Hutterites, and rarely by the larger public.

Through Plainspoken, readers outside their communities can learn what authentic Plain Anabaptist life looks and feels like—from the inside out. The Amish and Mennonites and Hutterites have stories to tell. Through Plainspoken, readers get the chance to hear them.

Author's Introduction

OUR TUESDAYS happened more by accident than by conscious planning.

There were five of us sisters growing up together with our four little brothers in the white farmhouse our parents built. This house is situated on the rise of a small hill, beneath the sheltering canopy of eight towering silver maples. Five of these trees line up along the front of the house; three more circle to one side.

The nine of us kept this five-bedroom house brimming with life and crowded with both happiness and some inevitable sadness. We did a lot of living and a lot of learning in that house.

And then we all grew up.

I was the first to leave. On a warm and sunshiny day in September 2000, after the leaves on the lofty silver maples had faded from summer green and before they wore brightly flaming autumn shades, I was married to Laverne Weaver. It was the first wedding in that mellowing white house we all called home. Four more were to follow in the next years.

We never sat down and planned for Tuesdays. But after I moved six miles away to my own home, I gradually acquired the habit of going back to the old home place and spending a day each week with my family. On Monday I always had laundry to do, as well as scores of other jobs to tackle after the weekend. And before Laverne and I had children, I worked part time in a bakery at the end of the week.

That left Tuesdays. Tuesday really was the perfect in-between sort of day to spend with Mom and my sisters.

Regina was married the following year; Ida Mae and Emily were both married in the spring of 2005, Ida Mae in March and Emily in April. And Amanda, the youngest of us five girls, also had a spring wedding in 2009.

In retrospect, it seemed the white house beneath the maples had emptied fast, and even our little brothers were little no longer. One had also gotten married, one was living in Alaska, and one was planning a spring 2017 wedding. Except for Christopher, the youngest of the nine of us, Dad and Mom were alone again.

Except for Tuesdays. On Tuesdays the five of us sisters still come home. We pack up the children—eighteen of them during summer vacation—and head to the farm. The large house snugged in by the maples is full again, and more than full.

We go early. I drive my spirited little mare, Charlotte, and she trots briskly along the six miles of winding country roads. Regina and Ida Mae live much closer. They married brothers, and their homes are directly across the fields from Dad and Mom's farm. They usually bike, with children's noses pressed against the bright mesh of the carts they tow behind their bicycles. Or they walk, pushing strollers over the back fields and up the lane. And Emily and Amanda, who also married brothers and live in neighboring houses about five miles away, come together with everyone crammed into one carriage.

The children love Tuesdays. On warm days they play on the slide and the swings in the cool shade of the silver maples, jump on the trampoline, run through their grandpa's three greenhouses, ride along on the wagon going to the fields, where produce by the bushels and bins is hauled to the packing shed. They build hayhouses in the barn and explore the creek. The boys take poles and hooks and bait and spend hours fishing and playing in the small creek that flows beneath the lane and through the thickets beside the pasture fence. They catch dozens of tiny bluegills and northern creek chubbs, most of which they release back into the water hole, a deep pool that yawns at the mouth of a large culvert, to be caught again next week. They work, too, at mowing lawn, raking, lugging flowerpots around, or anything else that Grandma needs them to do, but most often Tuesdays on Grandpa's farm are play days.

We don't exactly play, yet Tuesdays for us are also about relaxing. Of course there is always work to do—just making dinner for such a group is a big job—but the day is more about relaxing, reconnecting, visiting, and sharing. We talk a lot, we laugh a lot, sometimes we cry. Tuesdays is about being sisters, daughters, moms. It's about learning what is happening in one another's lives.

Every day is different, yet every Tuesday follows a predictable pattern that varies with the seasons. Winter finds us inside, close to the warmth humming from the woodstove, absorbed in wintertime pursuits, which include card-making, crocheting, sewing, doing puzzles—jigsaw, crossword, Sudoku—and reading books and magazines. But as soon as spring colors the buds of the maples with a reddish tinge, we spend more time outside. The greenhouses are loaded with plants, the flower beds full of unfurling perennials, and the grass is greening in the yard again.

In summer, while the garden and fields burst with produce, the breezy shade of the front porch calls. It wraps around two sides of the house and is full of Mom's potted plants and porch furniture. We sit there to shell peas, husk corn, or just sip a cold drink and cool off after a warm stroll through the flowers.

Then autumn echoes through the country, the leaves flame and fall, and we rake them up—millions of leaves. Where we rake one Tuesday is covered again by the next, until at last the towering maples stand disrobed of leaves, their amazing seventy-foot branches a wavering fretwork against a sky that is sullen with winter once more.

The years spin faster now than they used to, and we catch and retain only fleeting memories of the months as they come and go. Once upon a time there were nine of us growing up in the house Dad and Mom built to be our home. We have moved on, but what we learned there is with us still, and those things are alive and well and budding in the hearts of the next generation—the eighteen children who play and work and laugh and cry and generally fill our old home with new noise every Tuesday.

I watch the children at play and marvel at the heritage our parents bequeathed to us, which we in turn are passing on to their grandchildren, and I think about the lines of a verse I love from Psalm 16: "The lines are fallen unto me in pleasant places; yea, I have a goodly heritage" (verse 6).

The years go fast, it is true, but what is written down is never forgotten. These are fleeting memories of fleeting moments of a year of Tuesdays spent gathered with sisters, children, and Mom.

FAMILY MEMBERS

My family members including parents, my siblings, and our children.

Dad and Mom
- Darla
  - Cody
  - Alisha
  - Matthan
- Regina
  - Jerelyn
  - Lowell
  - Dean
  - Carrie
  - Corey
  - David
- Ida Mae
  - Bradley
  - Melody
  - Luella
- Emily
  - Tristan
  - Travis
  - Wesley
- Noah, married to Christine
  - Rosalyn
- Amanda
  - KellyAnn
  - Makayla
  - Janessa
- Nathan
- Anthony, married Norma
- Christopher

JANUARY

Tuesdays at Mom's and the Tuesday Tablecloth

THE CALENDARS have all been changed. A new year is like a new book. What do the pages hold?

It began to snow this morning as five-year-old Matthan and I were on our way to Mom's house, small flakes that meant business. Soon the world was a white blur, and we were wrapped in the middle of a quiet cocoon of softly falling flakes. It was rather like traveling through the middle of one of those snow globes we used to have when we were children, where a vigorous shaking started a mini blizzard.

The six miles Matthan and I travel to Mom's house follow a winding course through hilly back roads. Depending on whom you ask, these are either high hills or small mountains. I use the terms interchangeably. Whether hills or mountains, they are steep, with steep drop-offs that lack any suggestion of guard rails.

I began to worry a little about the dreaded snowplows, and fervently hoped we wouldn't meet any. Actually, I admire the dedicated people who work in cold and stormy weather to keep the roads safe. It's Charlotte our horse who doesn't like to see the thundering iron beasts approaching. She always practices some fancy dance steps when one passes, and I'm afraid that someday she will jump down over a bank.

There are banks along the winding ridge road over which I have no desire to tumble. A few have only a narrow shoulder—less than a foot wide—from where the blacktop ends and the hillside makes an almost vertical drop into deep and rocky gullies. If Charlotte ever took us down over one of those, it's highly probable that we wouldn't climb back up by ourselves.

Despite her dislike of snowplows and other unusual beasts lumbering along the road, Charlotte is a good horse. Laverne bought her for me to drive after I had a mishap with his horse, and I certainly appreciated the gift. I depend on her for at least a weekly jaunt. She's a pretty little mare just spirited enough to keep me on my toes when I'm driving her.

We passed the two most dangerous drop-offs along the hilltop road, quickly and safely, as we have hundreds of times before. Soon we were heading downhill, down off the high ridges we call home, to where the rolling fields of Mom and Dad's farm edge the road.

Their lane is rolling too. It rolls downhill toward a small stream of water, fed by a natural spring somewhere, that idles lazily through a culvert underneath the lane, and then the lane climbs again. Past the greenhouses, the other sheds, the barn, up the hill to the big white house beneath the silver maples.

The horse and carriage that Emily drives was already there when I arrived, and assorted bicycles and a stroller announced that Matthan and I were the last to arrive. We normally are.

In the L-shaped kitchen and living room was the Tuesday morning chaos of arrival. We each haul along a box or basket or bag of some sort—I use my laundry basket—with the items needed that day: work or crafts, food to contribute to dinner, the children's innumerable paraphernalia, and books and magazines to exchange. It takes a while to stow away coats, decide who gets which issue of what, and sort out what we have brought for dinner and plan a complete menu around it.

When I had my basketful of stuff emptied and sorted, I helped myself to coffee and sat down at the table. "Guess what the editor at Herald Press wants me to do," I announced when everyone was assembled. I didn't expect them to guess, of course. "She would like for me to do a book about a year of our days together and call it maybe *Tuesdays with Mom*." Reactions varied.

"I suppose you would change all our names," Mom said after a while.

That was a new thought for me, and one I didn't want to consider. "Oh, no, that would be much too hard. We would just use everyone's real name." Merely the thought of renaming eighteen children—nineteen counting my oldest, Cody—exhausted me.

"Maybe you'll have to Sunday-us-up a bit," Emily suggested with a laugh. "Make sure we all use our best manners when you write about us."

"Oh yes, I won't write anything you wouldn't like," I promised.

"She will still have to claim us as sisters," Regina pointed out, as usual finding a positive angle to the topic. "She won't make us sound too odd or ornery or anything."

I promised not to.

Regina's oldest daughter, Jerelyn, who at fourteen has graduated from eighth grade and is again spending Tuesdays with us, considered staying home for the entire next year to keep her name out of the book. But on the whole, no one really objected.

Like Laverne and our children, Mom and my sisters are almost used to my compulsive scribbling. Almost.

• • •

The forenoon hours were busy as usual as we prepared dinner. Today Amanda brought pizza supplies, so Mom mixed up a batch of dough, enough to spread over two cookie sheets. I had brought salad fixings, so while they layered on pizza sauce, sausage, cheese, and pepperoni, I chopped lettuce, grated carrots and radishes, added bacon bits and cheese, and tossed together a salad. Regina had brought some of her homemade baked beans, made with navy beans and limas, and that finished our meal.

While the pizzas baked we added extra leaves to the table and stretched it all the way across the kitchen. On Tuesdays it has to be lengthened to seat anywhere from about fifteen, in the winter, to its full capacity of twenty-four to twenty-eight—depending on how many children we can squeeze on the bench—in the summer. Even then, the older children have to take turns to fill their plates and eat picnic-style at a table on the porch.

We brought out the Tuesday tablecloth—so called because it's the only one long enough to cover the entire length of the stretched-out table. It used to be a bright blue green, with a pattern of blocks that has flower designs in the center, but it has faded over the years to a smoky blue. The squares still tumble over its yards, though, in various shapes and sizes, and the flowers still bloom.

• • •

I guess we sisters resemble the tablecloth a little bit. Over the years we've faded too. We've all added some extra pounds and wrinkles. Occasionally we commiserate with each other about a first gray hair, and glasses have become a reality, at least for me.

But those are simply the outward signs. In the fading years of youth we've matured—at least to a certain extent. We've added a few insights, gained some wisdom. The years have been kind for the most part, if relentless; and what we've lost of the bright merriment of youth has been amply replaced by the settled contentment of these full, ripe, mellow years lived alongside the ones who grew up with us and whose lives are forever entwined in the memories of yesterday.

• • •

The wind remained cold, but after dinner Matthan, Wesley, who's also five, and Corey, soon to be four, wanted to play outside. We bundled them into coats and beanies and sent them out. The snow had melted and the temperature was not quite freezing, and the noise level indoors is greatly reduced when even a few of the children decide to play outside.

Behind the house, in the muddy field, they found a patch of ice over a shallow ditch. It was barely frozen, but it made a fairly nice pond for the three little "skaters." They slipped and skidded back and forth, stumbled through the just-thawing mud beside it, and stamped holes into the thin layer of ice.

It didn't last very long. Soon there was a banging and a kicking at the door. When Emily opened it, there was our trio of little boys, wet to the knees and muddy to there as well. They were cold too, with hands and cheeks turned cherry red by the wind. They dropped their coats and shoes on the rug just inside Mom's front door—do they still not know any better?—and went to find something warmer to do.

Even the little girls wanted a breath of fresh air, so they went outside as well, to make mud pies in the cold January mud. KellyAnn and Melody have just turned six, and Makayla is four. They also came in soon, with coats and skirts streaked with mud and their hands caked with it. Even Makayla, who is otherwise a little lady, likes mud pies and mud puddles.

These are Matthan's Tuesday playmates—KellyAnn, Melody, Wesley, Corey, and Makayla. They are the six who fill Mom's house with noise and play and disagreements every week. Janessa and Luella, who are both turning three this year, play with them too, and baby David, Regina's youngest, watches everything with bright, dark eyes.

They play the hours away, but they disagree too, and their quarrels vary in degree from mild to serious. Matthan can be selfish and set in his own ways, accustomed as he is to playing alone at home, and it has been a good experience for him to be plunged into the midst of ready-made playmates just his age and size, at least once a week.

• • •

I had brought along dress patterns and three pieces of fabric. Two were to cut into dresses for my daughter, Alisha, and one was for my new dress. But after I finished washing the dishes, coffee and chocolate bars looked more appealing, as did a new book called *Dusty Rose*, which Mom had just bought to add to her library.

While my more industrious sisters cut patches for comforters to send overseas (Regina), crocheted a pair of baby socks (Ida Mae), and colored and cut stamp art pictures to make cards (Emily and Amanda), I was lazy. I am not into crafts, and neither do I enjoy buying fabric just for fabric's sake, as do the others. I buy just enough to keep Alisha and myself supplied with plenty of dresses.

But I laughed along with them when Mom produced a paper a friend had sent. She read aloud to us "Fifteen Reasons to Buy Fabric," from an unknown source. Various versions exist.

1. It insulates the closet where it is kept.

2. It helps keep the economy going. It is our patriotic duty to support cotton farmers, textile mills, and quilt shops.

3. It is less expensive and more fun than psychiatric care.

4. Because it's on sale.

5. Because I'm worth it.

6. A sudden increase in the boll weevil population might wipe out the cotton crop in the next ten years.

7. I'm participating in a contest. The one who dies with the most fabric wins.

8. It keeps without refrigeration, you don't have to cook it to enjoy it, and you never have to feed it, change it, wipe its nose, or walk it.

9. I need extra weight in the trunk of my car for traction on snowy, icy roads. This is important, even in Florida or Southern California—you never know when the weather will change.

10. Like dust, it's good for protecting previously empty spaces in the house, like the ironing board, the laundry hamper, the dining room table . . .

11. When a big earthquake comes, all the quilt shops might be swallowed into the ground and never be seen again.

12. Stress from dealing with the Fabric Control Officer (my husband) made me do it.

13. It's not immoral, illegal, or fattening. It calms the nerves, gratifies the soul, and makes me feel good.

14. Buy it now, before your husband retires and goes with you on all your shopping expeditions.

15. A yard a day is all the quilt shops of America ask.

Before long Matthan and Corey were both wailing and needed some attention. Their disagreement had escalated to the point where Corey whacked Matthan on the head with his toy giraffe. Matthan retaliated by smacking Corey on the head with his toy elephant. Both giraffe and elephant are large plastic beasts from Mom's assortment of zoo animals, and I'm sure the boys' heads must have hurt. Regina and I reminded them that Grandma's toys are to play with, not to use as weapons, and to share nicely. But somehow they no longer wanted to play with zoo animals.

Mom's sixtieth birthday present to herself arrived in the mail as a belated gift that day. It was a laminated song calendar, like a daily calendar with pages to flip. Soon we were humming and singing snatches of songs. "Prayer Bells of Heaven," "Beautiful Home," and my favorite, "When We All Get to Heaven." We sang the chorus together: "When we all get to heaven, what a day of rejoicing that will be! When we all see Jesus, we'll sing and shout the victory!" I can usually carry a tune when someone else is also singing, and I croaked along with my more musical sisters.

Soon another joyful noise drifted to our ears. An uneven line of children had congregated before the sink—KellyAnn, Melody, Matthan, Wesley, Corey, Makayla. Even Janessa and Luella had found places in the row. They each clutched a picture book—holding them right side up, upside down, and sideways—and they were singing in a lovely clamor of voices, noises, and sounds. There was nothing bashful about them, and their joyful noise sounded just as beautiful as ours.

• • •

I skip a Tuesday at Mom's house only about four or five times a year, and last week had been one of those times. Matthan had thrown up all night and was still quite a sick little boy who lay on the recliner all day long instead of joining his cousins at Grandma's house.

But now it was Tuesday again, and he thought it had been a very long time since his last day at Grandma's house.

"Or did we skip a Tuesday?" he asked.

"We sure did," I replied. "Don't you remember? You were sick and didn't feel like going anywhere."

"But I didn't know it was Tuesday," he said, and his tone implied that had he known he would certainly have crawled off the recliner and gone.

Because it was a rainy morning, Alisha needed a ride to school first, and I scurried around to be ready in time to take her along. It was also my turn to chauffeur the neighbor children, so we picked up five of them along the winding gravel road to school, and they crowded into the carriage with us. The carriage door was being stubborn; either it would refuse to budge or it would fall off. We were crammed suffocatingly together, and the blankets became wet and muddy from even more wet and muddy boots and from the rain shivering in through the crack of the stubborn door.

Alisha was feeling snappish by the time Charlotte halted near the schoolhouse door, and so was I. There the carriage disgorged six children, and I sighed with relief. (The carriage may have too.) Matthan and I found a nice, dry spot on the blanket, and Charlotte jogged off to Mom's house, relieved to have discarded some of her load.

Rain fell all day, shutting us up in the cozy house, where the woodstove hummed a winterish tune and the children played with a relish and a racket. We chopped potatoes and carrots, browned beef and onions, and made a beef noodle stew for dinner. It was the perfect meal for a cold winter noon.

When it comes to quarreling, and sometimes fighting with words, fists, and tears, Matthan and Melody win all the prizes. KellyAnn is a peaceful kind of little girl who is seldom involved, while Melody is a spirited lass who clashes with Matthan. One of their disagreements a year or two ago ended with Melody flouncing over to Ida Mae and saying, "Matthan won't go with me to *my* school, will he, Mom?"

But today when Matthan fell off the bench at noon and bruised his cheek, Melody was most sympathetic. Matthan wept long and loud and shed many tears, and all the while Melody was busy carpeting the library floor with all the soft blankets she could find. "It's a surprise for Matthan," she explained. "If he's hurt he needs something soft."

I don't know how blankets on the library floor were supposed to assuage his pain, but in this case it was the thought that counted. And Matthan was happy with the idea when

Melody and KellyAnn invited him to the library. He perched on the chair and began auctioneering. Over the next few minutes he sold dozens of books to Melody and KellyAnn.

. . .

Anthony, our second youngest brother, gave his fiancé, Norma, her engagement present on New Year's Day. I don't know where the custom of giving a clock for engagement originated, but in our community it's a long-standing tradition. Those clocks are special and cherished for years, often a lifetime.

"April," Anthony said when we sisters wanted to know the date they had chosen for the wedding, and that's all he would say.

I suppose it was to be expected. Anthony likes to tease us. It must be payback time for him, and now he's getting revenge for all the times we bossed him when he was younger.

Not that his refusal to reveal the day made any difference to us. We began immediately to discuss the details—sewing new dresses from the fabric they had chosen, who would oversee scheduling a bus to take us to Pennsylvania where Norma's family lives, what wedding gifts to buy, and whether the men and boys needed new white shirts or if they still had some good enough for a wedding.

As sisters of the groom, we get the fun and specialness of a family wedding without much of the hassle and stress and headache of planning it. Weddings normally take place at the home of the bride, and preparations for services, guests, and the wedding meal take much planning and attention to detail. And that's in addition to cleaning the house, readying the premises to host all the guests, shopping for vast amounts of food, and making sure there are enough of all the many supplies that are

needed. Besides this, Norma will have wedding songbooks copied that contain the songs they have chosen, will create keepsake samples made with fabric from her wedding dress and the
other wedding colors, will make menu sheets for all the cooks
and table waitresses, and will attend to dozens of other things.

So we still didn't know when the wedding would be, but the
fabric that Norma chose for us to use for our dresses had arrived at Mom's house over the weekend. I found my bag in the
large box and stowed it in my basket to take home. There were
eight yards of material: four yards for my dress and another
four with which to make Alisha's. This would be enough, and
some left over. The "some sort of blue" that Anthony described
as one of their wedding colors turned out to be a nice shade of
periwinkle.

"Nathan plans to come home from Alaska for two weeks over
the wedding," Mom said. We haven't seen him since October,
when he was home recovering from a twenty-five-foot fall from
a roof where he had been working. Seeing Nathan is another
reason to look forward to the wedding.

• • •

I made yummy filled cupcakes to take along this week to Mom's.
Or perhaps it would be more appropriate to say I tried. The
chocolate batter was so thick that it plopped into the cupcake
papers, and the cream cheese filling stayed on top, rather than
sinking into the center as a filling. It oozed brown and sticky
over the top while the cupcakes baked.

Thinking over the recipe ingredient by ingredient, I realized I had probably forgotten to add the final cup of water to
the batter.

Disgusted with my cooking ability—or do I mean disability? —I tossed the cupcakes into a pan and hauled them along. Everyone is used to my flops.

Amazingly, today I wasn't alone. Emily removed the top from her pan of donut bars and said in disgust, "What a flop I made of these. I would have left them at home if I had realized how bad they would look by now." She replaced the top, but not before we got a glimpse of bars hilly around the edges, large holes sunk in the centers, and the frosting melted off. The bars and the cupcakes made an interesting dessert at noon, anyhow.

Amanda placed three tubes of refrigerator biscuit dough on the counter when she arrived. The change in temperature must have caused the dough to rise, because some time afterward we all jumped when a sound like a gunshot exploded behind us. Biscuit dough ricocheted against the ceiling and tumbled down again.

• • •

There are few things Mom enjoys as much as planting flowers, and in the winter she simply moves her gardening indoors. Her rooms are full of houseplants.

African violets are by far the most numerous of one variety. The pots line the windowsills, and many bloom all winter; their ruffled little flowers, in every possible shade, add a cheery tint of color during winter's gray days. Orchids, ferns, vines, succulents, and many others are grouped in corners.

One part of the kitchen counter between the sink and the oven, beyond which are several windows, is what Mom calls her small nursery. Here she has dozens of pots of tiny violets, succulents, and other plants in various stages of rooting, or preparing to grow and thrive. When these are bigger and have developed healthy root systems, she sells them or gives them away.

"Real gardeners can't live without green, not even overnight," Mom said, quoting words from a story called "Peace, Love, and Peperomias" by Tovah Martin that was printed in the early spring issue of *Country Gardens* that had just arrived in her mailbox. "That pretty well explains why I have so many houseplants."

I realized again that my love for gardening and growing things is most certainly inherited—from both my parents. Come to think of it, I probably didn't have a chance. I was born already compelled by some inner drive to garden.

Dad and Mom taught us that life is formed of good and bad things, and it's up to us what we permit into our lives or focus on. For example, take dirt and mud. It's a part of life that you can't escape, at least not in the country. But you can plant vegetables and flowers there and grow a garden, rather than dwelling on the ugliness that can't be changed. It's true that sometimes, such as in winter like now, the mud is more apparent, but it's only for a little while.

Life, like each year, has its seasons, and as you deal patiently with winter—"patient in tribulation" (Romans 12:12)—it will eventually yield to spring.

Plants aren't the only hobby Mom has, for she loves crafts of any kind, and adult coloring books are the latest thing. I took two along today, one called *Colour Your Life* and one called *Colour Your Day*. They are full of Bible verses and illustrated with many flowers, birds, butterflies, cupcakes, kaleidoscopic patterns, and other everyday things, artistically outlined. I had told KellyAnn she could color a picture for me in each one.

KellyAnn and Matthan shared one and colored on the middle pages of the same book. Melody chose a page full of umbrellas in the second book, and transformed the black-and-white picture into a vivid and variegated rainbow of colors. Later that day she was reduced to tears when she discovered that Janessa had taken a crayon and added some colors of her own.

I joined them at the table and colored two pictures in one of Mom's books while Ida Mae colored another. Mom showed me how she uses some of her adult coloring book pages to make scrapbook pages to mail to others. I thought this idea had possibilities, even for someone as artistically challenged as me.

The backs of the colored pictures are blank, and after we have colored them, Mom uses that side to write letters to her mom, our grandma, who lives in Pennsylvania. That's why she always requests that we sign our name on the page when we finish. And after their names, the children usually add their ages.

Ida Mae watched KellyAnn carefully printing "age 6" and asked, "Do we have to write our age too, or should we add our weight?" Ida Mae is a few months into her fourth pregnancy and thinking about weight gain.

"If I have to put on my weight," I said, "is it okay if I just write what I wished I weighed?"

They all laughed. "What do you wish you weighed?" Amanda asked.

That was an easy question to answer. "What I weighed on my wedding day."

We all agreed. What we weighed on the day we were married would be an ideal weight. We were all quite a bit thinner then.

Regina, who enjoys scrapbooking the way I enjoy writing, had enlisted our help to make a calendar for one of our aunts. Her birthday was coming up in February, and Regina wanted it to be ready by then.

"Sorry to torment you like this," she said to me in a tone that suggested she wasn't sorry at all, "but I want the calendar to be from all of us. So you will also have to design two pages. Only Christine [Noah's wife and our sister-in-law] gets away with doing just one."

My sisters all like scrapbooking, and so do Christine and Norma. I long ago resigned myself to being the odd one out. They all have stampers and ink pads and Big Shot machines and colored pencils and scores of other things for which I don't even know the name, all pertaining to making cards and scrapbooks.

I sipped my tea and tried to look moderately intelligent while they discussed what designs and shades and poems they would use on their calendar pages.

"Darla, I have a rose stamper you could use to make a border on one of your pages," Regina suggested. "Unless you would rather do something else."

"I'll need all the help I can get," I predicted grimly. Art of any kind is just not my cup of tea. But a rose page sounded sort of nice. I decided I would make one for Aunt Edith's calendar.

The first five words in the Bible are "In the beginning God created." Our God is a creative God, as is so evident in the vast diversity of the amazing universe he designed to be the home of his crowning glory, which is each person with a living soul. And I believe that into each soul is infused a seed of that creativity, that desire to create, which is unique to each one. I sometimes gaze at the stamped creations my sisters design and marvel at the talent required to do something like that, for it's one I lack. I would far rather plant gardens or write stories, and that is all right. We all express our own creativity in the way God made us.

• • •

Regina and her family had visited friends in New York State over the weekend, and Corey had learned a new game, which he now wanted to teach his little cousins how to play.

Melody agreed to be the first monkey. She wore a pile of hats on her head, and her eyes sparkled with mischief as she paraded around, trying to sell them to the four other monkeys, who were Matthan, KellyAnn, Wesley, and Corey. "Sixty cents a hat," she sang. "Sixty cents a hat."

None of the other little monkeys seemed interested in purchasing a hat, so at last Melody gave up. She sank down beside a chair, laid her head against the seat, and pretended to go right off to sleep.

While she slept four little monkeys crept up one by one, and each of them stole a hat off her head before scampering away.

So convenient was Melody's sleep that she awoke immediately after the last one departed and discovered that only one hat remained on her head.

"Give me back my hats," she cried, leaping to her feet. She was shaking her fist and trying to look angry (while her eyes sparked laughter and her smile spread wider).

KellyAnn, Matthan, Wesley, and Corey bounced around her, hissing and shaking their fists.

"Give me back my hats!" she hollered, stamping her foot. The four other monkeys laughed and hissed and stamped their feet.

"Give me back my hats!" Melody shrieked, really trying to appear cross, but failing. She threw the last hat still on her head down to the floor.

Four more hats hit the floor near her feet as the other hissing little monkeys imitated her. Melody swooped down and snatched up all her hats. Now she had a stack to wear on her head again.

The children loved this game and played it over and over. Each one wanted a turn to be the monkey wearing the big pile of hats. For a while as we went about our work we were kept busy dodging all the hats that sailed around the kitchen.

• • •

I mixed up a batch of pizza dough before I left home this morning, and it jiggled around in my laundry basket for the six-mile carriage ride. It was a sulky-looking mass when I arrived at Mom's house, but I kneaded it into subjection, patted it flat on a cookie sheet, and raided Mom's cellar for a jar of cherry jam.

I spread the jam down the center of the dough and used a scissors to cut two-inch strips along both edges. These strips I folded in over the cherry filling to form a braid. It still looked amazingly nice when Regina decided it was finished baking.

When it was cool I drizzled glaze over it. But I left the cookie sheet on top of the oven where Mom's cornbread was baking for dinner, and the glaze melted and slithered to the four corners of the cookie sheet. And I should have used pie filling, which would have been thicker. The jam was too runny; when we cut the braid, thin rosy filling mingled with the glaze and oozed everywhere.

Also, the glaze had a strange smell. The first bite tasted like sour milk, but I hadn't used any milk to make it. Amanda and I sniffed, tasted, and peered at it, but we couldn't figure out what might possibly be wrong.

"Never mind," I said, resigned. "I know I can even flop the unfloppable."

Mom had made a big kettleful of chili, baked a large batch of cornbread, and opened a jar of bread-and-butter pickles. Regina had brought a chocolate cake, and Ida Mae a cream cheese dessert. There was plenty to eat anyway.

So soon it was time to gather our things together and go home. The last Tuesday of the first month of the year was already gone.

I recalled words from Deuteronomy 26 about rejoicing "in every good thing." This, I think, is what we do when we enjoy with gratitude all the blessings God showers upon us and not think too hard about the burdens he sometimes asks us to carry.

• • •

"And thou shalt rejoice in every good thing which the Lord thy God hath given unto thee."

DEUTERONOMY 26:11

FEBRUARY

No New Shoes for Mama

RAIN POURED DOWN as Matthan and I left home the first Tuesday morning in February. A rising wind lashed the tree branches above the lane and whipped up miniature waves on the many puddles of water that had appeared overnight in the fields and pastures.

Matthan sat on the carriage seat beside me, snuggled into the blanket. He never liked storms, but this morning he watched the water rilling down over the windows and tried to be brave. "God promised never to send another big flood, didn't he?"

"Yes, he did," I reassured him.

Matthan considered that for a while. "Heaven will be so nice that we can't even imagine how it will be," he said next.

"Yes, that's true," I said.

"It will be even nicer than playing at a little creek with my water animals." Matthan's favorite times of late were spent playing with his new water animals. I agreed that it would be.

Matthan pulled a few of his tiny, treasured animals out of his pockets. "Maybe Wesley and Corey will want to help me play with the beaver and the otter."

"Last week Emily was sick," I reminded him. "Maybe Wesley picked up the germ and is sick now. Then he wouldn't come today."

Matthan pondered that between the space of a few of Charlotte's hoofbeats. "*Germs* isn't a very nice word," he said. "It's not an animal, but it sounds like something that would attack you." He made good sense. Germs do attack.

Wesley was not sick after all, as Matthan discovered when he ran through the rain to the house. I took care of Charlotte, pulled the winter blanket around her and fastened it to keep her snug, snatched up my basket, and dashed for the porch too.

Inside, all was cozy and noisy, and the cheery yellow flowers on the plastic table cover were all but obliterated by the things piled there. I set my basket on a chair to empty it.

For one thing, there are always magazines to exchange. One issue or another is constantly making the rounds. We each subscribe to the Pathway papers for ourselves individually, and then if we also subscribe to one other magazine and share it, we get to read all the usual magazines we enjoy without having to pay all the subscription rates. So it is that *Ladies' Journal, Keepers at Home, Written on My Heart, The Connection*, and *Shining for Jesus* (a children's magazine) are kept busy making the rounds for a month or more, and come full circle at length looking a little worse for the wear.

Ladies' Journal and *Written on My Heart* were both waiting for me, along with a stack of other magazines from Amanda. I slipped everything into the bottom of my basket and put it away. This forenoon I had to tackle another job.

"I have to plant my elephant ear bulbs today," I reminded Matthan, who was already playing with Wesley and Corey. "Do you want to come with me to the greenhouse?"

Matthan could hardly take the time to give me a proper answer, and I asked twice more. "Nope," he replied, without looking up. I ran through the rain, down the hill to the three greenhouses. My destination was the middle one, where my son Cody, who worked here two days a week, was busy potting Easy Wave petunia plugs. He looked up as I entered.

Rain spit on the roof in a pleasant rhythm, and the plastic on the greenhouse flapped in the wind. Droplets of moisture cascaded from the rounded roof with every undulation of the plastic; as I pulled the door shut behind me, the familiar greenhouse fragrance swirled around. Inside was stillness and cessation of storm.

I can never step into the warm, humid atmosphere of the greenhouse without remembering all the days I spent working there as a girl. The memories return; not as a single one, but as a tide of pleasant hours that passed long ago and are now recalled by the colors, scents, and sights of another season starting.

The long tables were full of baby plants just beginning to grow: pots of geraniums and ivies, flats of cabbages, trays of tiny tomatoes. Above my head, near the roof, dangled hanging pots of Boston ferns in double tiers, and large planters brimming with coleus lined the aisles.

I wandered through the greenhouse for a little while, looking for the old, familiar standbys, as well as for what was new this year. Fronds of wandering Jew and asparagus fern vines draped from the center row; impatiens and coleus cuttings filled dozens of trays; and succulents, a bestseller in recent years, filled a large section of another table.

A small calico cat padded soundlessly from beneath one table to weave around my feet, and when I came back to where

Cody was at work, I disturbed Sheba, the large and shaggy Australian shepherd, and she flapped her plumy tail at me but refused to budge from her spot near Cody's feet. These pets like the warm, moist heat of the greenhouses in the winter, and often sneak inside to doze under the tables near the heating pipes.

"Tell Jerelyn to come and help me," Cody said, "or she shouldn't get any dinner."

I promised to pass along Cody's message, then hurried to the other end of the greenhouse and out to the furnace room. As I entered, I inhaled the woodsy, slightly smoky air, with its scent of damp soil and wet, growing plants. It was time to get busy.

I opened a fifty-pound bag of Promix and dug my fingers into the soil. Then I started separating the elephant ear bulbs and filling pots. It was a yearly job, and one I undertook for two reasons: because the large elephant ear leaves are a favorite plant of mine for a certain shady corner beside my house, and because if I potted them now, the plants would have a head start for when I wanted to set them outside.

This year I had twenty-two pots. I carried them all into the greenhouse and lined them up on the floor beneath the center table along a heating pipe. I only needed five to plant at home, so if all of them grew I would have seventeen pots left to sell. Not bad for a few hours' work.

Back in the kitchen I found dinner preparations underway and everyone busy. Matthan and Corey were sitting in chairs and writing, pretending they were at school, while KellyAnn, Melody, Wesley, and Makayla were lying on their stomachs on the floor, coloring pictures.

Regina was coloring too, taking her turn to do a picture in Mom's book. "I was hiking on the Appalachian Trail this morning when it was time to get up," she remarked.

"Did you go off by yourself to do this?" we asked.

"Oh, no. Duane went along too, and we took all the children. It was a circus."

We laughed at the convenient way dreams have of making things possible that would be impossible in real life.

When we stopped chuckling about her dream we suggested it might be best to wait awhile before they tried more hiking with their family. "I think we will," Regina agreed. She reached for a pen to sign her name on the finished page.

"Remember to add your weight," Amanda reminded her.

"Maybe we should add our ages too," Emily joked. "It would help us remember how old we are from one day to another."

• • •

February is the month to finish extra sewing before the spring rush begins, and Ida Mae was cutting out pieces for a dozen prayer coverings from a yard of white material. Bonnets and shirts are some other items yet to be tackled this month by the seamstress among us, which is Regina.

I counted out quarters to pay Ida Mae for the two pounds of chocolate chips she had brought for me and reflected on how grateful I was that I could just buy bonnets for Alisha and myself, plus our prayer coverings, and pants for the boys. If a chart were kept that measured such things, my talent for sewing would be above my culinary talent, but not by much. I piled the shiny silver quarters on the table near Ida Mae's elbow. "For those chocolate chips," I explained. "Or won't quarters work?"

"We do like hundred-dollar bills better," Ida Mae admitted.

Emily and Amanda were both doing a bit of hand-stitching on the capes for their dresses to wear to the wedding. "A bus is finally scheduled for a two-day trip the last week in April," Emily said. "The only reason we got it even then is because another trip was canceled the day after we called. So they called back and told us the bus was available after all, if we still wanted it. It has been a genuine headache to find one still available. But the Oberholtzer bus out of Shiloh is free for the days we want it."

"That's good news!" I said. We reflected on that blessing and were grateful indeed.

• • •

Our conversation rambled on in haphazard fashion as dinner-time came and went. It covered a wide range of unrelated topics, including how to can red beet juice so it won't turn brown in the jars, how to package the calendar we finished, which was now ready to mail to Aunt Edith for her birthday, and how spoiled today's children are when it comes to food.

A few weeks ago Emily had brought carrot sticks for dinner, sliced from carrots that were still in her garden. Melody took one look at them and exclaimed in disgust (and to Ida Mae's dismay), "I can't believe anyone would expect us to eat carrot sticks without any ranch dressing to dip them in."

Today Amanda brought carrots, plus dip. "Here you go, Melody," she said. "The girls and I thought of you while we were making this dip!"

Dishes are another big job, considering the amount it takes to feed everyone. We take turns to wash them, but currently we are skipping Amanda's turn. She is due to have a baby next month and doesn't fit at the sink so well anymore. We made sure she sat down and propped up her feet instead.

That meant it was my turn to tackle the heap of dirty dishes, and I plunged right in. I do all disagreeable jobs just as fast as I can to get them over and done. Just before I finished, I took the trash outside to empty it into the compost bin. The rain had stopped and there in the grass were the first few purple crocus buds.

So soon it will be spring again, I told myself. Winter was already on its way out the door.

• • •

I had brought a dress along to hem, and I worked at that after the dishes were done. Normally I would set my sewing machine to the blind-hem stitch at home, but today I decided to do it by hand while I was at Mom's and save some time when I got home.

The day remained windy and became even warmer. By one thirty the winds were increasing, and they roared gale-like through the bare branches of the silver maples. The high, blustering notes of the wind shrieking around the house made me nervous.

"Thunderstorms are predicted for later this afternoon and evening," Ida Mae commented. "Some of them are supposed to be severe."

That made me even more nervous. I finished stitching up the hem of my new dress and gathered my things together, preparing to head up the hill. If I left earlier than usual, I hoped I might reach home before the predicted storms arrived.

"Get your coat and hat, Matthan," I said, when I had everything packed into my basket. "It's time for us to go."

"I don't want to go home yet," he protested. "It's not time. I don't want to leave first."

I insisted, however, and Matthan's frown soon covered his whole face. He sat beside me on the seat and sulked while KellyAnn, Melody, Wesley, and Corey ran along beside the carriage for a short distance on the circle drive.

"Goodbye, Matthan," they called, waving and smiling. "Bye, Matthan. Bye! Bye! Bye."

Matthan refused to wave back.

They spend a day together each week. You would think it shouldn't be so hard to persuade them that it's time to go home. But each one of the cousins has had many a turn protesting the day's end. Years ago, it used to be my older children whom I led to the carriage while they cried because they wanted to stay longer at Grandma's house.

These days the younger ones take turns. Sometimes it will be Melody, crying with a stamp of her foot, "It's not time to go home already." Or Corey wailing, "We don't want to go home now." Occasionally even KellyAnn takes a turn by protesting, "But we don't want to go yet."

Today it was Matthan's turn. He sealed up his lips and folded his arms and refused to say or wave goodbye, no matter how much the others waved and called.

• • •

February's usually unpredictable moods were running true to form this year, and the following week favored us with a mild

Tuesday. It was so mild, in fact, that Laverne helped me hitch Charlotte to the lightweight, two-wheeled cart.

Matthan and I weren't quite alone that morning. He often fills his pockets with his latest treasures to take along, but this week his newly acquired and much-loved possession didn't fit into his pocket. It was too long and too wiggly. That's why a very realistic and lifelike brown snake was riding along in my laundry basket.

Matthan had discovered that snake at Dollar General a few days earlier, and had fallen completely in love. He still had some Christmas gift money to spend, which was why he was in the toy aisle, and Cody was supposed to help him find something.

Well, in the end Matthan did his own finding. He was well on the way to following in the footsteps of his nature-loving daddy, and to Matthan's way of thinking it was not unusual to want to buy a snake.

I, on the other hand, felt dreadfully jumpy as I pushed around a shopping cart with a lifelike snake riding on top. It was so real I half expected it to start moving any minute, and I did my best to persuade Matthan to leave it in the store. The cashier, however, ignored my obvious revulsion, and handed the snake back to Matthan as soon as she had rung up the purchase. She appeared to think it completely normal for a five-year-old boy to buy a snake.

"I can probably scare KellyAnn and Melody with this," Matthan said happily.

I clumped to the house in the falling-apart shoes I was wearing while Matthan ran ahead, carrying the snake he liked as much as I hated it.

Ida Mae was the first to notice what he held. "Matthan," she exclaimed with some consternation, "I think you need to go home again."

Melody was holding baby David, and she didn't like it any better. "Take that snake away," she cried. "It's too real."

There were more exclamations of disgust from Mom and my sisters. I'm not the only one in my family who hates snakes— but KellyAnn seemed almost as fascinated with it as Matthan was. And Makayla held it gently to examine it in greater detail. So if Matthan still expected to scare the little girls, he was disappointed.

• • •

Almost every week during winter there's a new jigsaw puzzle on the board, and the one that greeted us today was especially charming. Five bright-eyed and ring-tailed little raccoons were nestled in a strawberry patch with pretty green leaves, red berries, and white blossoms, in the convenient weedless perfection of pictures.

After admiring the latest puzzle, I fixed myself a cup of coffee and clumped to the table in my aggravating shoes. It would feel good to complain a little, so I did. "Between paying for Cody's braces and food for Alisha's cats, there's nothing left to buy shoes for me," I grumbled. "See what I have to put on my feet? Shoes that Alisha wore to school until they were full of holes."

I didn't get any sympathy, just laughter. I think they weren't taking me seriously. Regina offered to bring me several more almost worn-out pairs.

I assured her I wasn't interested and sipped my coffee instead. Of course I could have bought another pair of shoes if

I absolutely needed to, but there were some other things waiting for attention first, if possible. People who write books, I reflected, don't have as much money as you would think. At least not in the beginning.

Sitting there at Mom's table, I suddenly wondered how our parents managed. There had been nine of us to provide for, after all. Nine to feed and clothe and shelter and educate, to say nothing of appointments with doctor and dentist and to keep supplied with shoes and soap and toothpaste and notebooks. There were some lean years with few extras, but on the whole I think back and remember being happy and satisfied and well cared for. How many sacrifices did our parents make for us? How often did they continue to wear worn-out shoes themselves to make sure we had what we needed?

Sitting at the table in Mom's kitchen for a while has a way of putting things back into perspective and reminding me that holes in my shoes are a very minor blip on the screen of life. I cheered up. Or maybe my mood also had something to do with my having kicked off Alisha's shoes to walk around stocking-footed.

• • •

Christopher was home from almost a week of kayaking in the Everglades with a few of his friends. "How many pythons did you see?" I asked. Chilling tales of huge and numerous pythons in the Everglades had been a consoling send-off for the boys left behind.

"Not a single one," he replied, sounding disappointed.

"So you didn't even have a chance to use the machete you lugged along to use in case a python leaped into the kayak with you?"

Christopher laughed. "Nope!"

"Well, what about alligators? Surely you saw some of those?" Supposedly the alligators were even more numerous than the pythons.

"Just two alligators. When we rented our kayaks they told us to make a lot of noise and the alligators would leave us alone."

"So did they?"

"Well," Christopher said, "the one alligator that came close enough we poked with a paddle. When it didn't leave we whacked its tail, and it left fast. But that was while we were still on the docks. Nothing dangerous about it."

We asked what had been the most dangerous part of their kayaking trip. Christopher thought it over. "Perhaps the most dangerous thing we did was kayaking on the Gulf of Mexico one day. We were a long way out from land, between islands. If a strong wind had come up, that could have been dangerous. It would've been hard to get back to land."

That certainly sounded more dangerous than fun to me, but I realized that boys just turned twenty-one have a much greater sense of adventure than a middle-aged mom of three. The most adventurous things I do these days—sigh—is making sure I get Cody to his dentist appointments on time, fishing Alisha's old shoes out of the closet to slip onto my disgruntled feet, or pushing a grocery cart through Dollar General with a toy snake on top of the load.

• • •

There were three Lewis B. Miller books in my basket, and I carried them to the small room at the corner of the house, the one Mom has turned into a neighborhood library.

After we girls left home one by one and Mom finally had more space, she took this small extra room and filled it with shelves on three of the walls. It is crowded with books by the hundreds, and the neighborhood children for quite a few miles around diligently scour the shelves for new titles, or read some old favorites again.

Lewis B. Miller was an author from the second half of the nineteenth century who wrote dozens of frontier tales about when Texas was a wild and dangerous land, when Native Americans roamed the prairies and settlers pitted their resources and stamina against beasts, weather, hunger, and poverty. I slid the three books Cody had finished reading into the line of others on the shelf. I would let him choose the next titles he wanted.

The lowest shelves were full of picture books and easy readers and various series for younger readers. Gradually, the children's books made way for other reading—true stories and classics, fiction and nonfiction, old hardcover books, bright new paperbacks, garden encyclopedias, and magazines from bygone years.

It's a cozy and peaceful place, and I sank down on the cushioned chair that stood in one corner. The noise of the children already at play in the other room was muted and harmonious. There was a brown and beige rug on the floor, a potted tree wedged into a corner, and a basket overflowing with children's board books beside the chair. Nearby was a step stool to use when removing books from the top shelves.

In front of the single window was a small table where houseplants bloomed and returned books waited to be shelved again. A notepad was lying there, and on it people listed the books they were borrowing. Off to one side, on the floor, was a large tote bag full of extra books that were for sale.

I got to my feet again. The aura of peace here was refreshing, but conversation with Mom and my sisters was more stimulating. I went to the kitchen to see what everyone else was up to.

The children had set up a pretend meal with plastic food at their little toy table and were sitting around it in the small blue chairs. "It's Wesley's turn to lead the prayer," Melody said as I passed.

Amanda was combing her girls' hair, giving each of them sleek new braids. KellyAnn's hair is long and black, and her braids were smooth and straight and shiny.

Her eyes were shining, too, as she came over to me. "Did Matthan get an invitation to preschool days next week?" she asked.

"Yes, he did," I said. Matthan and KellyAnn would be starting first grade at the same school in September. Preschool days were held during the final months of a term, when the teacher invited the next group of first graders to come to the classroom for a few days. It gave them an idea of what would be expected of them the following term.

"KellyAnn has been waiting for preschool days for so long already," Amanda explained. "Now that she knows it's next week she thinks she can hardly wait until then."

Matthan was showing the others where he had lost his first baby tooth just a few days before. "Did you pull it out yourself?" someone asked.

"No. It was so loose that Cody pulled it out for me."

"Did you cry?" Ida Mae inquired.

"Of course not," Matthan replied indignantly.

Mom had a glass jar of dried sweet corn from last summer on the counter, waiting to be ground. I set up the small hand-operated grinder by fastening it to the edge of the table and prepared to pulverize the corn. When it was ground it would be ready to cook.

The first crunch of the grinder biting through kernels and the first rotation of the handle worked like the Pied Piper's music. In an instant I was surrounded by a circle of children. They sampled the corn, wobbled the table by climbing onto it, stuck inquisitive fingers too near the grinder, and reached for the handle. Each one begged for the first turn.

"You'll each have to wait for your turn," I said. "Let's see, Wesley asked first."

Even Luella climbed up on the bench. "I want a turn," she insisted. "I want a turn too."

Matthan was more interested in tasting the fragments of corn that tumbled into the pan than in turning the handle. Wesley stood on a chair, gave a few hearty yanks on the handle, and the grinder wobbled lose.

"Let me tighten it," I said. "Now try again, but rotate the handle backward for half a turn before you go forward. That makes it easier."

Wesley spun the handle backward for several revolutions. "It's easy now."

"Yes, but you're not grinding any corn," I said. "Turn it forward instead."

"It's my turn," Melody decided, bouncing around Wesley's chair. "Hurry up, Wesley."

Luella walked around the chair and back again. "I want a turn too. I want a turn too."

Before long they had each had a turn and had run off to play again. All except KellyAnn. She was still diligently rotating the handle. "You must like doing this," I remarked. "I remember the last time I ground some corn here and you helped me a long time. You did a lot of it too."

KellyAnn smiled. "I do like it," she said.

• • •

We started making haystacks for dinner, and there was plenty to do. We peeled potatoes to cook and mash, browned the meat and added seasonings and a can of beans, grated carrots, chopped celery and lettuce, heated cheese sauce. Mom sorted through the crackers and found a few packs to crush for the foundation layer of the haystacks.

Amanda's girls had brought loaves of bread that they had made themselves. Makayla's eyes sparkled as she placed her loaf on the counter, and Janessa was all smiles.

"We tried the bag bread recipe," Amanda explained. "The girls each made a loaf. We ate KellyAnn's for supper, and brought the other two along."

The bag bread was eaten with butter and plenty of strawberry jelly. The recipe is simple.

BAG BREAD

To start, give each child a gallon-sized resealable plastic bag. Into each bag put:

1 tablespoon active dry yeast
1 teaspoon salt
1 cup whole wheat flour

Close the bag and have child shake until well blended. Open the bag again, then add:

1 cup warm water
2 tablespoons oil
2 tablespoons honey

Close the bag and have child squeeze until combined. Open the bag and add:

1 cup white flour

Close the bag. Instruct child to knead the dough for 10 minutes. Then place in a warm area and let the dough rise in the bag until double in size. Remove from bag. Shape and place in a greased loaf pan. Let rise again. Bake at 350°F for 30 minutes.

Emily brought blueberry cupcakes for dinner, baked in brightly colored, reusable silicone cupcake "papers." "Cupcake papers that need to be washed?" Mom exclaimed. "What will they come up with next?"

"We found quite a few packs of them in the last load of surplus we got for the store," Emily said. "I can bring some along next week if anyone wants to try using them."

"Not for me," Mom said. "I'm too old to begin washing cupcake papers yet."

I was trying to decide whether I should ask Emily to bring some for me. In one way I agreed with Mom. Wash cupcake papers and make the pile of dirty dishes even bigger? And silicone in the food I baked? Wasn't it harmful?

But on the other hand, maybe I should save where I could. If I stopped buying cupcake papers maybe I could afford new shoes.

"Bring some along for me," Ida Mae said to Emily. "If the silicone doesn't poison me something else likely will."

I found I agreed with Ida Mae and said I'd take some too. Besides, everything keeps changing. Maybe by next year we'd find out that new studies had proven silicone is actually good for us.

The children weren't worried about silicone. They just liked the bright colors. They gathered up all the empty cupcake papers and made variegated stacks, alternating yellow, red, white, gray, blue, and purple.

After the dinner dishes were done, Emily and I went outside to work in the yard with Mom. We raked up the winter debris of branches and leaves that had accumulated beneath so many trees, and the bones the dogs had dug up.

It was so warm that the children came outside too. They dragged the large branches away from where we were raking and pretended they were horses harnessed to the tub we filled with raked-up debris, which they pulled to the burn pile. They hauled the branches down the hill to the barn and tossed them over the fence into the pasture.

Their noise and chatter brought a long line of curious heifers milling to the gate, their large eyes inquiring as to the meaning of this unusual commotion. Soon a line of children stood on the other side of the gate, peering back just as questioningly.

On the lawn beside the house, hundreds of crocuses had opened in shades ranging from pale lavender to deep purple. The children ran to gather the flowers, and Mom hurried after them. "The crocuses are full of bees," she warned them. "Watch carefully for one before you pick a crocus."

Sure enough, swarms of small bees swirled through the blossoms, enjoying both the nectar and the spring-warm day. Even the bees seemed to have forgotten it was still February.

A large clump of snowdrops was blooming in the flower bed that fronted the pasture fence. "I want to dig a few of those bulbs soon," Mom remarked as we stood there admiring the gallant white flowers. "Arlie [a neighbor] would like to have some, and I want to plant a clump at the house where Anthony and Norma will be living."

"They are really nice," I said, hinting shamelessly. "I don't have any snowdrops either."

"Oh, well if I remember I'll take some bulbs out for you too."

I haven't a single idea where I'll plant them, nor know why I think I would need another flower. But I'll figure out where to put them later.

When the raking was done and we were settled in the kitchen once more, Mom unearthed two bags of candy. One was filled with gummy life savers, and the second bag was full of red and pink gummy hearts, strongly flavored with cinnamon. The taste was so strong, in fact, that after I ate some I warned the children, "This candy is so cinnamon-y it almost seems to bite you back."

One by one they sampled the cinnamon hearts, rather gingerly at first, then with more enthusiasm. They poured the contents of the bag out on the table and helped themselves. It was candy after all, and they liked sugar.

"I like these," Wesley decided.

"So do I," Matthan agreed, picking up several more hearts.

The candies were almost all gone before the flavor got the best of them. Matthan came to me with a strange, teary look on his face. "This candy is too peppy," he complained. On the table were the slimy red remains of his last cinnamon heart, chewed up and spit out.

"You need a drink," I said, getting him a glass of water.

He ate no more candy hearts, but started licking up the sugar on the table that had spilled from the bag. I shooed him away and wiped it up with the dishcloth. It didn't seem to me that he needed any more sugar just then.

• • •

By the time we were ready to go home the middle room was more of a wreck than usual. "Who made such a mess?" Ida Mae asked, beginning the task of setting it to rights.

"Not me," Melody protested.

"Not me," Matthan echoed.

"Not me! Not me. Not me!" ran in a chorus around the circle of children who were staring at the disorderly room as if they had never seen it before.

I brought a broom into the room and set to work. "Evidently Mr. Nobody lives here too," I observed.

If nobody had wrecked the room, then everybody wanted to help clean it up. The children busied themselves putting away toys, setting chairs right side up, and picking up books.

I swept up potting soil from a spilled plant, picked the sofa pillows off the floor, shook off the rug, and stepped on a wasp that was alarming the children by being very much alive and crawling over the floor. The room was soon looking much better and we were ready to go home.

It was raining by then, and Charlotte was cross about heading out into the wet, rainy world. She charged out the lane, shaking her head and putting back her ears and making me wish she had more work to do and more miles to go. Winter was making her fat and sassy.

Each time a vehicle passed, spitting water from beneath the tires, she shied away, jumped, and charged on again. Even the hill didn't seem to tire her, or maybe she was too cross to care. Whatever the reason, she had cranky fits all the way home, either about things passing on the road or about things, real or imagined, that she saw beside the road.

By the time we got home I felt like having a few not-so-mild cranky fits myself. But we were home safe and sound, and Charlotte and I calmed down again. I breathed a prayer of gratitude—both for the day and for the safe journey home.

• • •

"The Lord shall give that which is good."

PSALM 85:12

MARCH

Do Horses Have Hormones Too?

MARCH WAS DOING its lion-est best on the first Tuesday of the month, with glowering skies, high winds, and sporadic downpours.

Because of the weather, Alisha wanted a ride to school, and I hurried to get ready to leave. She likes to arrive at school with plenty of time to spare. Unfortunately, we were unable to convey that same sense of urgency to Charlotte. She left her warm stall and ample breakfast unwillingly and dawdled along to school with a sluggish plodding that annoyed both Alisha and me.

Relieved to have Alisha at school on time and still dry, I turned Charlotte down the road toward Mom's house. Charlotte obliged in the same unhurried manner, making it plain she would rather go home instead. I relaxed. With Alisha at school, Matthan and I could let Charlotte choose her own pace and arrive when she at last meandered down the hill.

Past the potholes on Fairview Road, just where we did indeed have a long, fair view out over rolling blue ridges, a snowplow–dump truck combination swung round the sharp curve and hurtled past. What was a snowplow doing out in the middle of a March rainstorm? I didn't know and didn't stop to ask. I had a feeling Charlotte wouldn't like it any better in March than she did in January.

And I was right. Charlotte plodding and slow? Oh, no—she became Charlotte-very-much-alive at that point. Her first impulse was to slam on the hoof-brakes and dive into the ditch. That was impossible because I was stamping on the carriage brakes and hanging tight to the reins, so she satisfied herself with three short angry hops, after which she shot down the road in a fury for a short distance, then subsided into her pokey trot.

I was in a bit of a fury myself. Do horses have hormones too? I wondered. Or is she just tired of winter and cold and rain?

It was still raining lightly when I arrived. Matthan ran to the house while I unhitched Charlotte, and Christopher came to lead her to the barn. I was relieved. It would surely improve her humor if she was in the barn all day, staying dry and eating hay. I told myself she'd be nice and placid and easy to handle on the way home. (I am sometimes unusually optimistic.)

Near the house I was greeted by cheery yellow daffodils with centers like ruffled trumpets, the bright gold of miniature tête-à-tête daffodils, and the deep blue of tiny squills, all blooming in the rain and by all appearances happy about it. Follow the example of the flowers, I told myself. Let the rain pour, but be happy anyway.

• • •

I went to Mom's library to search the shelves for some Benjie books to read aloud to Matthan for his bedtime stories. Benjie is a little Amish boy who has many adventures and misadventures, and Matthan likes the stories. He especially likes the ones where Benjie's absentmindedness plunges him into humorous predicaments.

I was scanning the rows of books in case there should be any new titles I wanted to read, when a trio of grinning children tumbled into the room to join me. Their smiles were as bright as the flowers.

"Next week I will have preschool days at my school," Melody announced, her eyes fairly setting the room alight. "I can't wait. The days just don't go fast enough."

"My preschool day is tomorrow," KellyAnn said. "I will put an orange in my lunch box. And cheese curls. And a peanut butter and jelly sandwich."

I was holding *Benjie Goes to School* under one elbow and giving the children half my attention. "Oh, that's good," I agreed absently.

"I can't go yet," Wesley was saying with his unique lisp that still mangles a few of his consonants. "Next year I'll go. Then I'll be six, but I won't go right away."

His words "go right away" with *go* as the common euphemism for *die* (this was all in Dutch, of course) now had my full attention.

"But *you won't die right away*?" I asked in astonishment.

The children gazed at me with wide-eyed disbelief. "I won't go to school right away after my birthday," Wesley ventured a little doubtfully.

"Oh!" I exclaimed. "Now I understand what you said. Yes, you'll be six for a while before you go to first grade."

The children began to giggle and kept right on giggling while they looked at me. No doubt I had just made their day by my strange way of deciphering Wesley's lisp.

• • •

Melody brought along edible playdough shapes to share with everyone, and she passed the plastic container around for each of us to choose one.

"It's playdough you can eat," she explained, "but I didn't play with this. I just rolled it out and used my cookie cutters to make the shapes."

"I didn't think anyone would want to eat it if she played with it first," Ida Mae added.

"It would have gotten dirty," Melody agreed, pushing her container in my direction.

I picked out a tan diamond and took a bite. "Mmm, it's good, Melody. How did you make it?"

"It's not hard," Ida Mae replied. "Just mix two cups of powdered sugar with one cup peanut butter and one-half cup honey. It makes a nice dough. They can play with it as long as they like, or eat it right away."

We settled around the table to examine the cards Regina had brought along from a stamping party she had hosted the previous week and to discuss, among other things, whether pizza crust made with olive oil is tastier than pizza crust made with any other vegetable oil, and all the different variations of making bread sticks, and whether any certain way is superior to any other way. Our conversations rambled, as always, from one such earth-shattering topic to another and entertained us quite contentedly while the children played.

Or was it playing? They were running circles through the middle room, out through the kitchen, across the living room area, and back into the middle room. The noise level was high. It was way too high. They were making more noise than the six of us all talking at once, and that is saying something.

Matthan was begging to play with Mom's large bird book again, so Mom fetched it down from upstairs. This proved to be the distraction the children needed, and they settled down in the middle room, lying on their stomachs in a circle on the floor with the book in the center.

The book was big enough to accommodate them all. It contained a picture of every bird in the United States, and each had a number that, when pressed, vocalized the call of each bird. That's why Matthan liked it so much.

"I want to hear the woodpeckers," Wesley was coaxing. "Where are the woodpeckers?"

I flipped through the pages. "Let me check the index," I said finally. The seven hundred or so species were confusing me.

I found the woodpeckers for Wesley, and we heard the red-bellied and downy woodpeckers, which sounded familiar, and listened to the call of the ivory-billed, which we would likely never hear in the wild.

The children nicely took turns for a time, even showing Corey and Makayla which numbers to press, and the noise level was blissfully reduced.

Today I hadn't brought any work along, so when I found a new adult coloring book lying on Mom's sewing machine I decided to help myself to it. After all, there's nothing quite as satisfying as coloring that first picture in a brand-new book.

It was a large bouquet of daffodils, fitting for the day and easy to color. I selected the proper yellow and green colored pencils and set to work.

A bright bouquet emerged on the page as I colored. Not too bad, I reflected. The daffodils on paper were as cheerful as the real ones sashaying in the rain, pelted by raindrops just outside in the flower beds.

Melody peered over my shoulder. "I see one place where you colored outside the line," she informed me, as if she couldn't believe I had done something like that.

I sat back to inspect my almost-finished picture. "I could probably find a few more scribbles," I agreed.

Melody leaned closer to scrutinize my bouquet of daffodils. "One, two, three," she counted, pointing out each place where I had even a faint scrawl of color outside the black line. "Nine, ten, eleven."

Corey leaned around Melody and helped with enthusiasm. "Nine, ten, eleven."

"Eleven scribbles!" Melody cried, standing on the bench beside me, the better to broadcast this astounding bit of news. "I can't believe this. You made eleven scribbles."

"Fourteen, eighteen," Corey counted, gazing at me with disbelief. "Eleven, fourteen."

"Maybe Darla should go to preschool again too," Amanda suggested.

"It's really not that bad," I protested. "They're purposely searching for every tiny little mistake."

But Melody and Corey were really on the hunt, and they were not interested in my protests. Melody took the coloring book from me and went to show Ida Mae and Amanda all the dreadful errors of too-lavish coloring that, in her eyes at least, I had committed.

"Look at this," Melody cried, waving the book under their noses. "She made eleven scribbles. Even more, I should think, if I were to look for them. Like seventeen, eighteen, or even twenty."

Ida Mae studied the picture. "I think it looks nice."

"So do I. It's a very nice bouquet," Amanda said. "You don't see the colors that are outside the lines unless you really look for them."

I slid the yellow and green colored pencils back into the slender box and closed the flap. How like life that is, I mused. If you look for "scribbles" you can always find some. They are everywhere, the annoyances and irritations and vexations, the errors and mistakes and regrets.

And yet the beautiful, the blessings, and the benedictions are also everywhere for us, if we but choose to look for them and be grateful. Taken all together, when you step back and view life as a whole picture rather than seeing only its fleeting scribbles, it's often pretty nice. At least in many places.

And most often, we find what we look for in life. Or do I mean we get out of it about exactly what we put into it? "For as [a man] thinketh in his heart, so is he" (Proverbs 23:7).

• • •

KellyAnn rummaged through Mom's games and unearthed the ice cream game, which every one of the children wanted to help her play. The game had an ice cream scoop that flipped rotating colors, cardboard plates, and boards with pictures of assorted flavors. The children snapped the scoop, and when the color showed a certain flavor, they tried to find the matching ice cream boards to put on their plates. When the ice cream cardboards were all gone, the child with the most on his or her plate had won.

There were eight children, so they had to share the plates, the game not having been designed for that many children. They sat cross-legged on the floor or lay on their stomachs and proceeded with a great deal of racket that was happy to begin with but which quickly dissolved into quarrels and tears.

Emily got down on the floor to join in their game, and Ida Mae sat down on the other side. They straightened out the tangles, and with two moms helping, the game progressed smoothly to the end.

• • •

"Aunt Edith mailed a card and letter thanking all of us for the calendar we made for her birthday," Regina remarked as we did the dishes. "I'll have to remember to bring it along next week for you to read."

I plunged more plates into the dishwater. "She must have liked it."

"Oh yes. She wrote how perfect it all is, and what a good job we did on the pages."

I reflected that my page of roses had turned out halfway decent. And the second page—what had I eventually scraped together to put on that one? It was impossible to remember, but I didn't think it had been anything special. No doubt aunts were a little like grandmothers, and it was the thought that counted.

Matthan, Wesley, and Makayla pulled on their coats and went outside to play. They ended up at the bottom of the hill in one of the greenhouses with Grandpa. Here they soon found all sorts of treasures to drag back to the house. Matthan came in clutching a black plastic six-pack insert in his grimy hands. It really belonged in a tray, planted with flowers, but Matthan was using it to hold his treasures. In two of the cavities were snippets of a green vine, in two more were bits of grass, and the last two were holding tiny red begonia and petunia flowers.

"Because red is my favorite color," he explained.

Mom's dress for the wedding was finished and hanging over the shower rod in the bathroom. "It's done, except for pressing it," she said, "and to me that's the most dreaded part of making a new dress."

"I don't mind ironing new clothes," I commented. The ironing is a bit more complicated the first time, as the fabric needs to be moistened for it to be pressed permanently. "I actually sort of enjoy it. I could press your dress if you want me to."

"Go ahead," Mom said, sounding relieved. "It would be one less thing for me to do to get ready."

"Could you come press mine too?" Amanda asked jokingly. "I'm finished sewing all our dresses, but I haven't done the ironing yet."

"Would you do mine too?" Ida Mae asked.

"You could take a day off," Emily suggested, "and come to all our houses and press our new clothes."

I set up Mom's ironing board, put the irons on the gas stove to heat, and dampened a large green handkerchief to use as a pressing cloth. "I'll do your dresses, Amanda, if it can wait until we come to your house after the baby is born."

I laid Mom's dress on the ironing board. "But as for the rest of you, sorry, you'll just have to do your own. I'll do it for Amanda because she has three sets of wedding clothes to sew and iron this spring."

And I thought, but didn't say so aloud, that I was so glad I wasn't sewing for three weddings.

By the time I was finished laboring over the pleats in Mom's dress and pressing in several new wrinkles, which I then labored to press out again, I was glad I hadn't agreed to do everyone's dresses.

Wesley was driving a small tractor and wagon around in a circle, with Matthan riding in the wagon. They were happy making much racket of headache-creating decibels.

"I was talking to a lady the other day," Emily told us, "who said her mom had three boys first, and it made her loopy. She was never the same afterward. I wonder if it'll be the same for me. Sometimes I'm sure it will."

We laughed and assured her we had seen no signs. But then again, maybe we're all a little loopy by now. Middle age and motherhood have a way of doing that.

But boys do keep life interesting, I thought, and I wouldn't want to be without mine. Even if that sometimes meant eating breakfast with Cody to one side of me, wearing a big black fake mustache that he jiggled as hard as he could with each bite, and, on the other side of me, Matthan's toy snake wiggling through the legs of the chair.

Or being electrified when Matthan told me how smart he is. "Because I killed that ant before I ate it."

"You ate an ant?" I cried.

"Yes, and I killed it first so it wouldn't bite me back when it was in my mouth. Wasn't that smart?"

These three running around at Mom's house on Tuesdays, Matthan, Wesley, and Corey, are probably typical of most little boys everywhere. They love loud noises and mud and candy and toy tractors to ride. They keep life exciting for us, so who cares if we all become just a little loopy in the process of being mothers?

BETWEEN TUESDAYS

Early on a Sunday morning in March, Kevin and Amanda's little Ashley was born, joining her parents and her three sisters on March 12, 2017.

The thought of those four little girls stirred awake my memories of four other little girls who grew up together. One thing we never lacked was a playmate.

I remember faintly the years before school, which were spent on a little farm in Pennsylvania. I remember picking violet bouquets from banks starred purple in spring, making playhouses in the woods, taking wagon rides in the produce fields, sitting on the back porch to shell peas by the bucketful, and catching fireflies in the warm summer twilights.

Then there were the times we spent at the Susquehanna River, those long-ago afternoons when Dad and Mom piled all of us into the canoe and paddled to some distant island to camp out under the stars while the unceasing lullaby of the river sang to us all night long.

School days brought less freedom to run and play, but many necessary lessons. And it was during those years that we packed up and moved to southern Ohio, to the white farmhouse beneath the silver maples. I cannot remember that we had a hard time adjusting to a new home, and this was perhaps partly because we children were all still young enough that our immediate family was all we needed.

Then came the youth group years, and again our world widened rapidly. But everything is more bearable when shared with sisters, and share we did. We talked for hours about everything, both the frivolous and the important, as we tried to make sense of life and its complexities.

We shared our clothes too, which made for an extensive wardrobe. I remember eying a dress one sister was sewing and wondering how soon I could casually ask to borrow it for a Sunday evening with the youth group. Or wheedling permission from another sister to loan me her sweater for a weekend out of state. And shoes were another thing we shared. If the pair we wanted wasn't in one closet, it was likely in another.

Which stage in life was the best, and to which would I most willingly return? They were all good, and being middle-aged moms together on Tuesdays forges a still deeper bond. Who's to say this isn't the best time of all?

So I thought of Amanda's four little girls and I wished them the same deep bonds of sisterhood that I share with mine. I felt that I could wish few greater gifts upon them.

• • •

I was still not on speaking terms with Charlotte when another Tuesday rolled around. She had been in a worse-than-ever ill temper on the way home the previous week, ditching the carriage several times, or at least threatening to, such that I arrived home vowing not to drive her again for a very long time.

It was a dim, rain-misty morning, with occasional large drops of moisture slipping through the trees. I donned a yellow raincoat and put a bright orange safety vest over Matthan's coat before we set off on our bicycles. We never meet a lot of vehicles, just enough that we need to be careful, and the orange would help them spot us quite a ways off.

Matthan was fascinated by all the lakes, rivers, and waterfalls beside the road, which had been deposited overnight thanks to generous amounts of rain. "This is the best morning for us to bike," he assured me. "I like watching all the water beside the road."

"Yes, but it's more important to watch where you're going," I reminded him nervously. I was biking along behind him and making a general nuisance of myself.

"Watch out for that pothole, Matthan. A truck is coming, stay close to the ditch. Here's a steep drop-off beside the blacktop, go out onto the road a little farther. Don't look back when you hear that car coming up behind us. Here's another hill, Matthan. Should we get off our bikes and walk, or can you bike up this one?"

"Sure I can, Mom," he exclaimed, not in the least bothered by a little upgrade.

A dead opossum beside the road captured his attention next. "Just keep going," I advised, biking past without looking.

I wondered, as we threaded our way along those miles of winding country road, if there was a parallel here to how God watches over me on this road called life. Matthan was busy pedaling, and as long as he paid attention to my directions and warnings, I was keeping him safe, at least to the best of my very human abilities. I could see the ditches and the dangers and the things that might make him fall, things of which he was blissfully unaware.

I like to think that God is watching over me in somewhat the same way, yet even better, because he can see everything around me, behind me, and ahead of me. As long as I do my best to hear his voice and obey his commands, he can guide me through this life that has so many unexpected turns and unwanted detours. He can see where my path is headed. I can entrust my life into his hand, submit to his leading, and live in his presence.

Or I could take things into my own hands. I could bolt along in my own willful fashion and risk running off the side of the mountain.

All the way down the mountain I pondered the vastness in the almost insignificant daily choices we make, the often eternal consequences that begin with a single step on one path or another, the dimensions of a simple yes-or-no choice.

Matthan could choose to obey me, and I would do my best to keep him from falling off the road or getting run over by a car. Or he could refuse to listen to what I was saying, disbelieving that I could help him, and take the risk that he might not make it safely to his destination.

I guessed that my response to God could be much the same.

• • •

Mom had bought a book, *A Mother's Daily Prayer Book*, and showed it to Regina. "Is this exactly like the one I gave you not long ago?"

"I think so, but I can check." Regina leafed through the pages to a date in January. "Yes, it's the same book. This is the identical quote." She squinted as she read aloud a quote from Robert Louis Stevenson: "Then do not grasp at the stars, but do life's plain, common work as it comes, certain that daily duties and daily bread are the sweetest things in life." She looked up. "I copied this and put it on the refrigerator for us to remember, although the teenagers in our family don't like it so well."

"I think it's pretty good," I remarked. "But at fourteen I wouldn't have liked it so well either." At fourteen I also still wanted more excitement, more adventure, and a more interesting life. Now I find that the best and most satisfying things are the simple and kindly satisfactions of daily jobs well done, the contentment of serving and loving where God has planted me, and the quiet pleasures found in growing flowers, writing stories, and making our house a home to which we love to return. These years the things dearest to my heart are found closest to home.

Regina closed the book and handed it back to Mom with a sigh. "I don't like how much I have to strain my eyes to read these days," she complained. "And it has just begun in the last few months."

"Time for glasses," I suggested helpfully. "Do your eyes get dry and itchy and feel like they are full of sand or dirt by evening?"

"At least if you must wear glasses it hides the bags under your eyes," Mom said, intending to be consoling.

"You mean I have some?" Regina asked in a horrified tone.

"Now, you know I didn't mean that," Mom protested.

"Actually, she was looking at me when she said it," Ida Mae said.

• • •

I was sitting on Dad's favorite rocker with my feet propped up, browsing through the latest issue of *Country Gardens*. Regina had just finished feeding and changing David, and Melody saw this as her chance to rock him.

She lugged him in my direction. "I want this chair," she said, indicating the rocker. "Because Mom says I have to sit down when I hold him."

"Well, Melody," I said, reluctantly getting out of my chair, "I wouldn't do this for just anyone. But since it's you, and I like to write about you, I'll give you my chair."

"Are you making her the clown of the book?" Ida Mae asked. "Right now she doesn't care, but by the time she's fourteen she may thoroughly dislike you for it."

That, I decided, was a risk I had to take.

• • •

I brought several packs of little smokies along for dinner and wrapped the individual sausages in a thin strip of pizza dough before placing them on a cookie sheet to bake. Although I am culinarily challenged to a great degree, I do like making yeast doughs in general, and pizza dough in particular. This was a lengthy process, however, this wrapping of so many little smokies, and Emily kindly came to help me. Together we rolled fragments of dough into strips, circled each little sausage several times before pinching the edges together, and at last slid them into the oven to bake. It was tea party food, but one that could be served Tuesdays as well, and I rummaged through Mom's grocery shelves for barbecue sauce to dip them in.

"The bus has filled up fast now that the wedding date was announced," Emily said. "If anyone asks, there are only a few seats left anymore."

It was time to schedule pick-up stops, the time we preferred to leave for Pennsylvania, and the time of departure from the wedding. "Let's get an early start to Pennsylvania," Regina suggested. "We want to arrive in Snyder County about noon, or shortly after."

I agreed. "We'd like to have at least half a day to do some visiting and shopping."

"And we don't want to leave the wedding too early in the afternoon either," someone else put in.

"I'm hoping we'll have time to take our children to see our old home," Regina added.

"That would be fun. I wonder if we could go with you." I was thinking out loud.

We discussed, for a time, the question of lodging, and which cousins or aunts or grandmas we would ask to give us a bed for the one night we would spend in Pennsylvania, and whom we wanted to visit, and where we wanted to shop, and did I need to mention that Aunt Irene's bookstore was a high priority on my list?

After dinner I looked through a boxful of an odd assortment of things, which someone had disposed of by parking the box under our children's noses, thus exciting them by the idea of many treasures to be had for the grabbing.

Grab they did. I liked to think I was more discriminating, and I sorted out only the seashells. "To put around some of my houseplants," I explained.

"Some people are really weird," Regina remarked as she scrubbed the last of the dishes.

"Well, don't ask me to share any of them with you the next time you visit." I pretended to be insulted.

She just laughed as she finished rinsing the sink bowls. Then she hung up the dishcloth. "Before I sit down I want to run to the greenhouse and see if any new succulents have arrived. Maybe I can sneak a few pieces off some that I don't have."

This just goes to show, we told her, laughing, that people are weird in many different ways, and everyone is a little weird in one way or another.

Melody and Corey were lying on their stomachs on the floor, drawing on large pieces of paper, and Matthan and Wesley came to watch. Their watching soon turned into teasing, elbow joggling, critical remarks, and more noise. "Mom, the boys are bothering us," Melody wailed at last.

Ida Mae brought two more pieces of paper, one for Wesley and one for Matthan, and they settled down to do some serious drawing too. Soon there was a line of interesting pictures for us to admire, including a house that resembled a whale, scribbles that were intended to be a line with bunnies sitting on it, and a house surrounded by trees and flowers.

"Those are tulips," Melody explained. "Mom showed me how to draw tulips, so I made some of those."

We mentioned spending the following Tuesday with Amanda, a tradition we began when Cody was the newest baby in our family. Now we always spend a Tuesday together at the home of the sister who has had a new baby, before she feels strong enough to come to Mom's house.

"Plan a menu," someone was urging. "We have to decide what to take along for dinner."

"I could bake something," I volunteered tepidly, secretly wondering what that something could be and how it would turn out.

"I'll bring a pudding," Regina offered. "Our cow is giving lots of milk right now."

"I could bring a main dish," Emily said, "if someone would tell me what to bring."

"What about sandwiches?" Mom suggested. "We haven't had those poppy seed buns for a while. I could pay for the ham and cheese."

"I'll make them," Emily decided. "We can stop at JR's Store on the way home today. What would I need to buy? Two pounds ham and some Swiss cheese?"

"Let me make a salad," Ida Mae offered. Because of her gestational diabetes she is on a strict diet at the moment. "I'll fill a big bowl with lettuce salad."

The children brought out a long pink-and-green striped fabric tunnel and unrolled it across the floor. They were still crawling and rolling through its neon-colored length when it was time to put the toys away and get ready to go home. Not only were they crawling through it themselves and pretending to be puppies, but Matthan was trying to drive the little tractor and wagon through the fabric-covered hoops.

"Time to stop playing and clean up," we announced, heartlessly ignoring their protests.

Corey stood up in the tunnel and brought it upright, collapsing the hoops under his arms. Luella tossed pillows in to him while he dumped doll clothes over Melody.

"We're recycling," Melody explained.

"Who wants to buy me?" Corey asked. I wonder if he knows what recycling means.

• • •

Several large German shepherds, safely behind a fence, barked at Matthan and me the next Tuesday morning when we got off our bikes at Amanda's house. Emily's and Wesley's bikes were already there, so I thumped down a heavy hydrangea start beside Emily's bike and rubbed my arm. My bike box was full, so the bag had dangled from my handlebars for the last five miles while I held it in place. I was glad to be rid of it.

Everyone else had already arrived, and Matthan ran to join his Tuesday playmates at KellyAnn and Makayla's house. The children played with good high spirits all day long: swings, tricycles, and riding toys, and in the snug little playhouse the girls' daddy had built for them. And when all toys lost their appeal, they found mud and water, which never grow boring for children.

In the house we spent a slow-paced forenoon holding Ashley, trading news and various magazines and books, and getting dinner ready.

Both Emily and Amanda had recent letters from Nathan in Alaska, which we read. Alaska weather was still cold and snowy, according to his letters, with below-zero temperatures and snow measured in feet rather than inches.

"I went downtown to watch the Iditarod sled dog race kick off the other weekend," he wrote. "The race usually takes about two weeks to run, so we should know who the winner is by this weekend. Over the last five years the race has been won by the same guy or his dad, and it looks like the dad is going to win this year. It's funny, because it seems the race always comes down to the two of them, and they always finish first and second.

"At least they had snow for the Iditarod start this year. Last year they had to bring a trainload of snow from Fairbanks for the event. The start is in downtown Anchorage, about two miles from where I live, so I always go to watch it for a bit. It's only a 'ceremonial start.' The real race begins farther north the next day, and they start the teams at intervals, so it doesn't really seem like a race, but it's still exciting to watch. I guess because it's one of those things you can see only in Alaska. And it's crazy to think that the fast teams average more than a hundred miles a day."

"Nathan sent the boys maps of the race," Emily said as she began to cut apart the rolls for the sandwiches. "It showed the route from Anchorage to Nome. That's a long way."

"Does the Iditarod race follow the route taken by Balto, the sled dog?" Mom asked. "I just read a children's book about the diphtheria epidemic in 1925, and the dog who brought the medicine to Nome."

"We have that book too," I said. "*The Bravest Dog Ever: The True Story of Balto*. But I didn't know if the Iditarod follows the same route."

We discussed the possibility of the famous dog sled race having originated from the route Balto and the other dogs had taken. Our knowledge of Alaska, both historical and present-day, being sketchy, we thought it probable, but no one was sure, and life was full of more pressing questions and demands. Such as making sure some of the sandwiches had Swiss cheese and others provolone. And why was Janessa clinging to Amanda and refusing to permit any of her large and threatening aunts to braid her hair? And was there was enough mustard in Amanda's fridge to mix the sauce, or should Emily dash home to fetch hers? And would Ashley's eyes keep that dark blue color or begin to change, and did she look like any of her sisters or just like herself? And were her cheeks already fatter than the last time we had seen her?

The honey mustard ham sandwiches Emily made were delicious. The platters emptied fast. Here is the recipe.

BAKED HONEY MUSTARD HAM SANDWICHES

15 dinner rolls
1 pound sliced Swiss cheese
½ pound sliced ham
Topping
1 cup butter
⅓ cup brown sugar
1 tablespoon poppy seeds
2 teaspoons Worcestershire sauce
2 teaspoons honey mustard

Cut the rolls in half. Place bottom halves in a 9 x 13-inch pan, layer with cheese, then ham, then another layer of cheese. Place the top halves of the buns on top. In a small saucepan, combine the topping ingredients and heat until melted. Pour mixture over assembled buns. Bake at 375°F for approximately 20 minutes.

Mom was washing the dishes when Amanda brought out her little girls' dresses. "Do you still want to press these?" she asked me.

"Yes, I was planning on it." I put aside the dish towel I was using to dry the dishes and turned my attention to this other job.

The four little dresses hanging in a row made a pretty picture. They were a periwinkle blue, with a matching pale blue, flower-patterned apron, and ranged in size from KellyAnn's six years down to baby Ashley's tiny dress for her to wear when she would be almost seven weeks old.

I heated the irons and set to work, moistening the fabric with a spray bottle, pressing out wrinkles, pressing seams flat, pressing down pleats. It took a while to do all four, but at last they were hanging in a row again and ready for the fast-approaching wedding day.

• • •

After dinner, the children dragged toys and child-sized camping chairs across the backyard to a small creek that formed at the culvert when it rained. There they splashed, fished with sticks, and pretended they were camping.

Before long loud howls erupted from their camping area. Wesley had tumbled into the creek and was none too happy about his sudden bath in March rainwater. Melody ushered him inside before his tears had quite ceased.

Amanda took one look at him and said, "I guess you'll have to wear a dress now. I don't have any pants your size."

"I told him his mom could probably run home for some dry clothes," Melody said helpfully.

When it was time to go home, the children had discovered a large pile of unshelled corn in the barn. They were shelling some of the ears and throwing the kernels into the pasture for the goats, who seemed less than enthusiastic about it.

Ida Mae went outside to call Melody, and through the window I watched Matthan and Wesley run to their bikes clutching several ears of corn. It seemed they'd found another treasure. "But they'll have to put that back," I said.

Ida Mae came back inside, laughing. "KellyAnn told the children they could each have three ears of corn to take along home because her dad is planning to buy some more anyhow."

Amanda laughed too. "In that case, let them keep their corn." So it was that when we eventually left for home that day,

Matthan's three precious ears of corn were also trundled along in the box snapped into the carrier on the back of my bike.

• • •

"Great peace have they which love thy law."

PSALM 119:165

APRIL

Biking through Puddles: Spring Comes to the Hills Again

THOSE OF US who live in the country cannot help but be affected by the carousel of the seasons. Our lives revolve along with them.

About April, the pace of the year picks up, and outdoor work begins. But this spring continued to be rainy and wet, delaying garden planting and lawn mowing.

Skies were overcast when Matthan and I set off the first Tuesday morning in April, and I packed a change of dry clothes for him, just in case we were drenched by an April shower. We pedaled along together, skirting the puddles on the lane, and later the ones on the road.

At least I—mindful of the casserole strapped on the top of my bike box with a black bungee cord—steered around the edges of the puddles. Matthan drove directly through the middle. The higher the spray arcing behind his rear tire, the greater his delight.

But it was a pleasant ride. We were serenaded by spring peepers and red-winged blackbirds. The grass on the verges was emerald green and lush with spring growth, and underbrush was taking on a filmy chartreuse haze. A day of sunshine would have leaves bursting. Spring had come to the hills again, and everything was pulsing with life, color, and song.

Matthan was less concerned about the seasons. He was remembering the dead starling he had found in the grass under the maple trees several Tuesdays before.

"I'm going to see if I can find it again today," he told me. He loves all birds, even dead ones.

"That was two weeks ago," I replied. "I wish you would forget about that dead bird. It will likely be gone by now."

"No, it won't." Matthan looked serious. "I hid it in a little hollow hole in one tree so I can find it again."

"Please don't play with it," I begged. "By now it will be falling apart and yucky."

By the time I got to the top of the hill at Mom's house and parked my bike beneath the silver maples, Matthan had already been exploring. "I found my dead starling," he said. "It's still in the tree. Do you want to see it?"

I didn't, but I delayed unpacking the contents of my bike box and followed him to a tree behind the swing set. On one side a large branch had been lopped off near the ground years earlier, and a cavity had formed in the side of the tree. I peeped in reluctantly.

All that was visible were a few black feathers sticking up from the dark hollow.

"Nothing to play with anymore," I observed with relief. Matthan's arrival had amused Mom, who watched him from the window. "He pushed his bike up the hill and along the edge of the puddle beside the redbud trees," she told me. "He stopped and looked at the water, then backed up his bike, got on it again, and pedaled right through the middle of the big puddle."

"He biked through all the puddles between here and home," I responded, thinking about the splashes of dried mud on his clothes.

Shortly after I arrived, Emily and Amanda came. It was baby Ashley's first trip to Grandma's house; she was three weeks old. KellyAnn beamed as she carried her baby sister inside in a bundle of blankets. Amanda unwrapped them, surrounded by a circle of watching children. Ashley slept on, manipulating her pink pacifier and unconcerned about all the racket around her. She was wearing a cute pink sleeper, with a pink rose print, and she looked exactly like one of the little girls' dolls.

• • •

We were discussing again, endlessly, the myriad details involved in taking so many people five hundred miles to attend a wedding, when Christopher came in the door.

"By the way, Christopher," Regina said, "I hope you won't marry a girl from out of state. I'm not sure that I could ever again manage to get my family all that way to a wedding, plus see to all the details of clothes and gifts and lodging, and everything else required."

"I've already told him he's not allowed to notice any of the girls in Snyder County," Emily said. "I never again want to oversee chartering a bus and arranging all the details of pick-ups and drop-offs."

I decided this would be a good time to add my two cents' worth. "I don't really care where she comes from," I assured our obliging littlest brother (who's taller than any of his sisters). "All I'm concerned about is that when you ask a girl you give her a fair warning. If she marries into this family she will probably be written about at some time or another. Make sure you tell her that soon. If not on the first date, then shortly afterward."

"While she can still decide to run away from us if she wants to," Amanda put in.

Truly, being a younger brother on Tuesday at Mom's house is not for the faint of heart.

"That poor girl is being written about before she even knows she is one of us," Emily said.

• • •

For dinner we had my casserole, a macaroni salad, and a pack of little sausages submerged in Sweet Baby Ray's barbecue sauce and baked for thirty minutes. We put a cake in the oven at the same time, and Mom rummaged through her grocery shelves and emerged with a can of orange candy corn frosting to spread over it.

Melody was not impressed. "This icing is so awful I can't eat it," she announced at noon after taking a bite.

It took our usual long discussion to decide whose turn it was to wash the dishes. (Why is it so hard to remember back to one week ago?)

"I think it must be my turn," Ida Mae decided at length.

"Me will rinse for you," Luella offered.

"I will rinse too," said Makayla.

"I want to rinse the dishes," said Corey and Janessa at the same time.

"You'll have to take turns," Ida Mae warned them. "I don't like fighting. If you quarrel, I'll send you all out the door."

Melody came running over and tried to quarrel with Corey, who only grinned good-naturedly. "Now I'll go out the door," she giggled, and her eyes laughed too.

Matthan and Wesley came back to the table while I was still clearing it; evidently they didn't share Melody's abhorrence for orange candy corn frosting. In fact, Matthan was indulging his colossal sweet tooth with several massive pieces, and Wesley was half out the door with his.

I made a grab for Matthan, who had a piece of cake in each hand and was scattering crumbs over tablecloth and floor. "On a chair with you, and there you stay until you're finished eating cake." I surveyed the orange smears on his face, and his sticky hands, and went to moisten a washcloth.

"But Wesley's going outside to eat his," Matthan whined.

"Oh, no he's not," Emily said. In a moment our two little boys were settled at the table with their crumbs and frosting smears.

Amanda came back from rocking Ashley and stared at the pieces of cake the boys were devouring. "I hope you left one piece for me."

They assured her that there was plenty left, gulped the last of their slices, whipped the washcloth in the general direction of their mouths, and dashed out to play.

Somewhere they found Christopher, and he gave them both a box and unlimited access to last season's leftover multi-colored flint corn. They set about filling their boxes, and soon Matthan and Wesley staggered up the hill to the house, where they played all afternoon with their corn. They loaded it into the little wagon they pulled behind the toy tractor and hauled it from room to room, stashing it here and there in imaginary barns and fields.

We spent a pleasant hour around the now-shortened table. Mom brought out a pile of greeting cards and we rooted through baskets of craft ribbons, stickers, and other card-making supplies. Makayla, Luella, and Janessa found some music buttons they liked, and KellyAnn discovered a little box stuffed with tiny appliqué-type flower patches. She laid them out in tidy rows. "I'm having a yard sale," she explained to Corey, who sat on the table, watching.

When the mail came there was a Great Lakes daylily catalog to dream through. The new selections were eye-catching and reminded us that daylily season was not far off.

Mom coaxed the first smiles from baby Ashley as we sat there, surrounded by a circle of amazed children delighted to witness this remarkable event. They didn't realize how short the years had been since each of them had also taken that first Tuesday outing to Mom's house. Nor did they realize how soon Ashley would—Lord willing—run after them all.

• • •

Wesley ventured upstairs, and in one room he discovered a doll wearing a little black felt hat with a black elastic band to go under its chin. He carried the doll downstairs, along with a pleading expression. "I like this little hat. I wish I could have it."

"That little hat is cute," Mom agreed, lifting it from the doll's head and examining it. "And it's more than fifty-five years old. When your grandpa was a little boy, Wesley, this was his hat. His mom gave it to me and I never could quite part with it."

"It's a keepsake," Emily explained to Wesley, "and not a toy or a doll's hat."

Wesley looked disappointed. "It would fit me."

Mom slid it onto his head and it was a perfect fit. "It's just the right size for you. Would you like to wear it home today?" Wesley's dark eyes began to sparkle at the thought.

"I guess we could bring it along again next week," Emily said, a little doubtfully. "If he got to wear it once he would likely be satisfied."

Wesley was happy with the plan. The little black hat fit on his head, the elastic was snug under his chin. He ran outside to find his grandpa. "Look, Grandpa. I'm wearing your hat."

"My hat?" Grandpa was surprised.

"From when you were a little boy," Wesley added.

"Wesley has taken a liking to that hat," Emily explained. "We'll bring it back next week."

• • •

I had resolved to be more forgiving, and that included Charlotte's quirks. Also, Laverne had given her an attitude adjustment in the form of three lengthy trips around the community. A bit more work has a way of trotting the mischief out of a horse.

It seemed to have worked. Charlotte was nice and placid and handled well, and we trundled off to Mom's house accordingly. I was copying a mental list into my memory. "Remember to buy seed potatoes, onion sets, cabbage, lettuce, broccoli, and cauliflower plants."

It was garden planting time, and the woods were veiled in the pale green of young leaves. The redbud trees were at their most splendid. Every branch and twig was dripping with pinkish-purple blossoms, and the dogwoods were coming on with masses of cream-colored flowers.

I sang "This Little Light of Mine" for Matthan as we followed the mountaintop road through trees and fields. "This little light of mine, I'm gonna let it shine, everywhere I go . . ."

Singing that song reminded me of another one Mom used to sing to us, called "Jesus Bids Us Shine," so I caroled that one too, although I make no claims of being musical. Matthan gave me an embarrassed glance. Then he climbed into the back seat of the carriage and watched the passing woods, ignoring me. I sang on: "Jesus bids us shine with a clear, pure light, like a little candle, burning in the night."

I liked the last line, "You in your small corner and I in mine," and repeated it several times. Sometimes I look around at all that is wrong and realize again there is very little I can actually do to make anything better, or even much improved. But I can shine in my one small corner, I thought, and there I can serve God faithfully at my simple duties.

• • •

The silver maples budded out into young leaves, and their towering limbs seemed to be wearing a misty green gauze that brushed the sky. Lilacs bloomed in every corner, and as I walked to the house I sniffed the fragrance that perfumed the air. On the side cabinet in the kitchen was a big bouquet of them: Sensation, with its purple flowers edged in white, and pale, double-blossomed ones called President Lincoln.

Mom had a stack of small bright blue plastic buckets, each with its own shovel and rake, that she passed out to the children. "One for each family to take along home," she told them.

The children immediately vanished outdoors into the warm April sunlight. Matthan and Wesley began to excavate around the base of a flower bed. "We're making a pond and a stream," Wesley explained.

"Share your bucket and shovel and rake with Luella," Ida Mae called after Melody as she and Corey carried their buckets outside. But before long Luella was inside again, tangling herself into Ida Mae's skirts and whining. Ida Mae went to investigate. "Melody, aren't you sharing with Luella?"

"Well, no, I'm sharing with Corey. He's using my shovel."

"I thought Corey has his own shovel and bucket," Ida Mae said, puzzled.

"He does," Melody explained, "but he's using mine instead. He put his away because he wants to keep it nice and new."

By the time I came outside there was a circle of children around the base of one of the maples. They were digging in the soil, scratching away grass, framing stick houses, and giving their imaginations a chance to thrive. "I guess there's no chance they can dig out that tree," I thought, and left them to their play.

I pushed the lawn mower to the circle drive, primed the engine, and started mowing. The grass was thick and heavy and sprinkled with white petals that had drifted like snowflakes from the ancient gnarled apple tree beside the lane. The thick clumps of grass toppled away beneath the blade, and I moved on to the hill that sloped to the greenhouses.

I enjoyed the job, the spring-fresh scent of newly mown grass, and the warm sunshine. Cars were coming and going at the greenhouses, and customers carried away vegetable starts, hanging baskets, and flowers. Teams were working in the fields, with the horses' harnesses jingling, as Christopher and Regina's husband, Duane, readied the soil for planting. April was the prelude to summer's hectic pace.

• • •

Emily brought along a brown-haired, brown-eyed doll she had found at a flea market. "I bought her to put with my toys," she explained. "But after I took her home I happened to see the writing on the back of her neck." She lifted the fringe of dark hair to show Mom the words engraved underneath. "This is a 1979 Madame Alexander doll."

"Then she is certainly a collector's item," Mom assured her. "I would have to check in some of my doll books, but I'm sure she would be worth something."

"She's yours if you want her," Emily said. "I just bought her for children to play with, and I don't want to put a collector's item in the toy box."

"I have a new doll upstairs, still in its box, that you can have for your toy box," Mom said. "A 1979 Madame Alexander doll is worth a lot. You're right, she shouldn't be in a toy box."

Ida Mae looked at Regina, who was born in 1979. "Would you be worth a lot too, I wonder?"

"Mom," I said, remembering to finally ask the question for which I needed an answer. "What's wrong with my African violets if they grow into a high pile of leaves, just in the center of the plant?" Several of mine had been looking increasingly odd, with small leaves clumping together in the middle of the pot instead of forming a healthy plant.

Mom has grown African violets for as long as I can remember, and knows about most of their diseases and peculiar little traits. "It could be cyclamen mites that are causing such a deformed plant," she suggested.

"Cyclamen mites?" I repeated. "But I've never seen any bugs."

"Oh, you won't see them. At least, not without a magnifying glass," Mom said. "But if you want to get rid of them you can take the plant and cover the top of the soil with a cloth to keep the Promix in the pot, then submerge the entire pot in a hundred-and-twenty-degree water. You'll have to keep the water at a hundred-and-twenty degrees for twenty minutes, which means you have to keep on adding hot water. And when you do that you have to be careful not to scald the leaves while pouring more water into the pan."

I continued to look less than enthusiastic.

"But if I know you," Mom went on, glancing at my face, "you would be more likely to throw those plants into the woods instead."

She knows me too well. "I certainly would."

"The mites are curable," Mom said. "But there's a virus that can affect the plants, and that isn't. Then you would have to get rid of all the plants. If you have a problem with mealy bugs or rust diseases you can always spray . . ."

Just about then I was thinking it would be easier to pitch all the plants into the woods. I could open a window and hurl them down over the mountain. I would never miss them and there would be less watering. The idea definitely had possibilities.

We made shepherd's pie for dinner, which is meatloaf pressed into pie plates and baked as a crust into which we spoon hot mashed potatoes and top with cheese. Everything is heated together just until the cheese is melted.

We baked dinner rolls too, and they were warm and fragrant. Butter melted on the steaming, just-baked dough, and dark purple grape jelly in glass dishes waited to be spread over the butter.

Corey liked his roll too, but for another reason. He kneeled on the bench behind the table and held his roll in one hand, drawn back behind his head and poised to let it fly. "I have a corner ball," he announced, mischief in his smile. "I like to play corner ball." He looked ready to begin.

Then dinner was over and all that was left was a big stack of dishes. I washed them fast. A walk down the hill to the greenhouses was next on the agenda, and I wanted to go along.

The vegetable starts were on outside tables, and I filled a tray with lettuce that was dark red and ruffled, as well as several kinds of cabbage (which no one at my house really appreciates), at least eighteen stalks of cauliflower, and a dozen of broccoli. Next I wanted fifty pounds of seed potatoes and two quarts of onion sets. This is surely the year the children will all love eating vegetables.

I loaded everything into the carriage, thinking as I did so that tomatoes and peppers and zucchini and cucumbers and lots of flowers would wait till another week, and possibly I could slip in some eggplants somewhere, and weren't the dahlias and gerbera daisies looking fine, and how many begonias could I plant this year?

I always go a little crazy when I'm planting things in the garden again. I love the new, healthy plants, still disease- and bug-free. Often by the end of a long season I'm tired of so many growing things to care for. But never in the spring.

Lilac Hill was scenting the air, so we went there too. The bushes were heavy with pyramids of blossoms. A huge bush with old-fashioned lavender flowers dominated the slope, and

the other bushes grew in a three-quarter-moon-shaped cluster around it. Miss Kim was there, Beauty of Moscow, Charles
Jolie, and various others in shades of deep red, white, purple.
Some had single flowers and some held double flowers that
looked like tiny roses. Columbines and violets bloomed in the
open areas beneath the bushes, and the children had already
been playing there on the shady, leaf-mulched hillside. A little
blue bucket hung on a branch, and faint trails were worn into
the mulch.

• • •

Back in the house again, we left the door open and sat down for
an hour of visiting before the day was over. Summery sounds
drifted in. The wind in the maples and the songs of the birds
mingled with the noise of children, calling and talking and
laughing as they played on the porch and in the yard under the
trees. They were still happy with all their little buckets.

Ashley woke from her nap and snuggled in Amanda's lap,
looking alertly at all of us with her big eyes, and appearing for
all the world as if she were wondering at the sort of aunts she
had acquired through no fault of her own. Her cheeks were
smooth and chubby, and one of them had a dimple. She looked
serene and content.

Amanda was browsing through a *Stampin' Up!* magazine
a woman had given Mom the previous week. "And when she
found out I had five daughters, she would gladly have given
each of you a magazine," Mom said. "I finally persuaded her not
to give me so many. I told her we would share this one, and that
you already have plenty of stamping supplies."

"Do we ever," agreed my card-making sisters.

Amanda showed a page in the magazine to Mom. "But if you feel like ordering something from her, you may buy this set for us to use," she suggested with a smile.

I flipped through the magazine too, admiring the artistic displays without understanding how they were designed. "We age not by years but by stories," I read aloud from one page. "If that's the case," I warned my long-suffering sisters, "I'm planning to really age you this year."

Melody ran indoors, lugging her plastic bucket. "I made a poppy seed cake," she explained, tipping the bucket close to my face. She had filled it with moist soil and decorated the top with small greenish lumps. "See? There's my cake. I used these for poppy seeds." She pulled up one green blob, which turned out to be a seed pod, one of thousands that would soon drop from the branches of the maples.

"Yes, indeed," I said. "You made a very nice poppy seed cake."

She ran out the door again, and was back shortly, this time with violets. "Lots of violets are blooming out here."

"I've been adding them to salads this spring," I said. "I chop up lettuce and spinach, and then we sprinkle violets on top. It makes a pretty salad."

Amanda tasted one of Melody's violets, but cautiously. "They don't have much flavor," I added.

"I've read that both the flowers and the leaves contain lots of vitamin C," Ida Mae said, sampling one too.

Melody came in eating a violet. Janessa trailed after her. "Are my teeth yellow?" she asked Amanda.

Amanda examined her teeth. "No, Janessa, they aren't yellow. Why do you ask? Have you been eating a dandelion?"

Janessa smiled, looking a little sheepish, and didn't reply. But she picked up one of Melody's violets and ate it. "Are my lips purple?"

Amanda laughed. "No, Janessa, your lips aren't purple."

"We tried something new this spring too," Emily told us. "We pulled up some sassafras roots when we were in the woods looking for mushrooms the other day. We used them for sassafras tea."

"How did you make it?" I asked.

"I didn't have any directions so I just guessed," Emily replied. "I boiled some water and added the roots after they were scrubbed, then we let it set a long while before straining it."

"Did you add sugar?" Ida Mae asked.

"Yes, of course. Lots of it," Emily said, laughing. "And it made a good tea. We all liked it."

In desultory fashion we discussed the upcoming school picnics—one is held at each school at the end of the term—and what we were taking. At length, as most of our conversations that month tended to do, we rambled on to the wedding the following week, which reminded each of us of all the work that still had to be done before then. Tuesday was almost over and it was time to move on again.

"So the next time we'll see each other," I said just before we left, "will be when we get on the bus next Wednesday morning."

And here's where the difference between moms and their children became most apparent. While the children would have yelled and whooped and jumped up and down and begun counting "how many sleeps," the moms groaned, thinking about all the details to be managed and the many chores and much packing to do before then. And only when we finally plowed through all the last-minute have-to-be-dones could we sink gratefully into those cushioned bus seats amidst those dozen-and-a-half giddy, cheering children.

BETWEEN TUESDAYS

Four months of planning and preparing had culminated in this moment of rocking gently down the highway in a bus full of family and friends, with a dawn of pastel splendor in the sky ahead. We were going east, back to what was and always would be our first home—where memories began. I was born in Liverpool, Pennsylvania, and my remembrances are rooted deep in the soil there.

But actually, this moment had begun earlier, at approximately two thirty when the alarm clock woke us and we staggered out of bed, bleary eyed but determined, and prepared the last-minute things.

Then Laverne, Cody, Alisha, Matthan, and I loaded our bikes with duffel bags, backpacks, pillows, and an accumulated mountain of paraphernalia that was somehow essential to a two-day trip, and readied for our two-and-a-half-mile bike ride to our pickup place at our nearest schoolhouse. The winding road was shadowed black by crowding trees, but the sky was powdered with stars and the bike lights blinked and pulsed. Matthan pedaled along rapidly and with entirely good humor, humming as he went.

Noah and Christine and twenty-one-month-old Rosalyn were already waiting at the schoolhouse. We locked our bikes in the basement and joined them on the porch steps to wait for our ride.

Almost as soon as we were settled a muffled rumble started in low and grew in decibels. It was our bus, lumbering up the steep Dry Bone hill. It creaked to a stop at the end of the school lane with a hissing of air brakes, and the lights came on. Luggage compartments were opened to stow our duffels and backpacks, and we carried bags and totes along to our seats.

After two more stops, the bus was filled with people. We were on our way, except that it was a jerky detour through winding back roads to the highway, and progress the first hour was slow.

The children were lucky. They curled up in their seats with their pillows and blankets and settled down to finish their broken night. Except the ones who were getting carsick.

"I'm going to tell Christopher to make sure he keeps his wedding in Ohio," declared my brother-in-law whose children were throwing up.

"Yes," agreed my brother Noah from his seat across the aisle, "all this ruckus to get one brother married off."

This sentiment could certainly be shared by Nathan, who was back from Alaska, about four thousand miles one way, and was heading to Pennsylvania with us on the bus. No one had traveled farther for this wedding than he had.

Daylight was coming and sunrise was closer. I could see well enough to write, so I rummaged through my tote bag for my notebook and pens, first sneaking a glance to check that some of my brothers-in-law weren't watching. But they had taken seats a safe distance away from me.

They don't know that when I travel I pack a notebook and pens as automatically as I pack snacks and water bottles (today I forgot the water bottles), and they might think I was writing about them.

Of course, today they might have been right.

• • •

All around me the bus was waking up. There was the rustle of bags, a muffled buzz of many conversations, the cries of babies protesting the trip, the laughter and chatter of excited children. Sleepiness had fled with the darkness.

We got breakfast at Eat'n Park Restaurant, and headed deeper into Pennsylvania, through the mountains and high ridges of Somerset County. Groves of redbuds formed a pink sea, and deep emerald mountain laurel bushes hugged the hills.

As on every trip east, the tunnels beneath the mountains on the Pennsylvania Turnpike were a source of thrills for the children, counting down the miles. Their excitement upon first glimpsing the small black hole yawning beneath the mountain always led to someone asking, "Do you think our bus will fit through that little hole?"

And the children always shrieked a laughing reply: "Of course!"

Bright lights in the tunnels under the mountains lit up the bus and created a swirl of color. Tuscarora Mountain Tunnel passed, and Kittatinny Mountain Tunnel. In the middle of Blue Mountain Tunnel we caught up with and passed a white van, and recognized other Mennonites from our home community. The windows of the bus filled with waving hands, and we reflected that the world is not as big as we had thought, after all.

• • •

The next day dawned foggy and cool, with mist drifting in off the Susquehanna River not far away. Tulips, azaleas, redbuds, and Virginia bluebells were blooming in the front yard at Norma's Pennsylvania home when we arrived, and the yard was full of people. It looked as if we had found the right place for the wedding of Norma and our brother.

A large white tent was set up for the wedding services, and the cooks and table waitresses were in the house, busy preparing the noon meal, which they had waiting for us when we returned to the house after the services. We began with dinner rolls, ham balls with pineapple glaze, cream cheese mashed potatoes topped with browned butter, and various other dishes, and finished with a chocolate and vanilla layer cake, ice cream, and coffee.

After the wedding party's table had been cleared, Cody, Lowell, Jerelyn, and Alisha, being gift receivers, carried all the gifts downstairs for the bride and groom to open. After that there was more visiting, and then singing in the tent for everyone who wanted to join in.

We were still singing when Matthan charged into the tent in a frenzy of excitement. "The bus came!" he cried. "The bus is here already." The long-planned trip and time with family seemed much too short.

There followed the confusion of loading forty-plus people with much luggage and many assorted bags, boxes, bundles, coats, and children. But at last we were all back in our familiar seats, and the bus wound through the rolling Snyder County hills down to the highway. By the time the nose of the bus was turned toward home beside the Susquehanna River, the sun was shining on the gently tossing waters. The children, three to a seat on the river side of the bus, pressed noses and hands to the windows and watched for the miniature Statue of Liberty we would soon pass.

I settled back into my seat. The fleeting hours had been filled to the brim and had passed too quickly, but now it was good to be heading west—going home.

Just in front of Laverne and me, Matthan and Wesley turned their seats into an Old MacDonald farm with plastic toy animals. The schoolboys returned to their favorite travel game of watching license plates on the other vehicles on the highway and keeping a list of all the different states they saw. Farther back in the bus I heard Jerelyn and Alisha singing "Twinkle, Twinkle, Little Star," and the hum of conversation swelled along the rows. The little boys around me were demanding food.

Snacks came out of the bulging bags: apples, bananas, popcorn, chips, nuts, cookies, and candy. That satisfied everyone for a little while. But not for long. Little boys (and girls) have an enormous capacity for storing away food. Soon they were calling out again. "Mom, I'm still hungry!" "I need a drink!" "Daddy, I want something to eat."

"Here's some candy. Share with the other children."

Sharing, to a child with a bag of candy in his hand, doesn't mean quite the same thing as it does to the parent. Soon there was another protest.

"Mom, Wesley won't give me any of his Skittles and you told him to share."

"But I'm sharing with Makayla, and she wants some more of them," explained Wesley.

"Mom!"—this from the swindled brother who was peering with outrage into the red Skittles bag he had taken— "Wesley left just three Skittles for me."

"I need something more to eat," said another disgruntled child.

He was amazed to hear his mom reply, "We don't have much anymore. Your uncle ate it all."

"But, Mom, I'm still hungry."

We passed huge fields of blooming mustard, and it was like earthbound sunlight spilled across the soil in great yellow waves. Matthan and Wesley knelt side by side on the seat, hands and noses against the window glass, to watch the passing flow of traffic and fields. Later they quarreled, and Wesley moved across the aisle to Bradley and Makayla for a short spell.

Bradley was keeping his nose glued to the window on his side of the bus, hard at work listing license plates, and Makayla had a pen and tablet. She was patiently filling the pages with doodles and scribbles and drawings, ignoring the schoolboys' noise as they called back and forth.

"Do you have Illinois?" "Hey, Bradley, I have twenty-four states now." "What's that one? Is it Texas?"

"Yep, yep, yep!"

KellyAnn and Melody shared a seat and a fat little children's songbook, and they were singing, quite appropriately, "The Wheels on the Bus Go Round and Round."

In the seat ahead of them Ashley wailed in unhappiness while Amanda changed her from her little blue wedding-day dress to a pink sleeper, and Melody stuck her head between the backs of the seats. "Now we're going to sing, 'The babies on the bus go wah, wah, wah!'" she informed Amanda.

"The mamas on the bus go sh, sh, sh!" sang KellyAnn.

Matthan and Wesley were auctioneering now, and Matthan stopped long enough to look back at me between the narrow space in the backs of the seat. "They could also sing, 'The daddies on the bus just read, read, read,'" he said.

I smiled and agreed, although this wouldn't have been as appropriate, for Ashley was soon sound asleep in her daddy's arms as he gently bounced her.

Bradley had been so absorbed in watching for license plates that his eyes were drifting shut. Soon they closed all the way, and then he sagged sideways and slept soundly. When Carrie came along the aisle with a bag of candy from Mom to share with everyone, he slumbered on.

"He would want candy," Melody said. She decided it was her duty to wake him, and cried in his ear, "Wake up, Bradley, there's some candy for you."

Traveling and a wedding had left Bradley exhausted, and he didn't stir. Melody shook him and pummeled his arm and shoulder. "Bradley, wake up!"

He never stirred, which showed how tired he must have been, and Melody gave up at last. "I guess he won't wake up," she decided, and she was right. He didn't.

Melody wasn't a bit tired, and after a while she was absorbed in her little tablet and pen. Soon she brought it to her uncle Duane. "I wrote a poem," she explained. "You may read it."

Duane took the tablet and inspected the lines full of crowded scribbles. "Oh, a nice poem about horses," he said.

"No!" Melody shrieked in protest. "It's a little poem about farming. When you've read it, Noah may read it too." (Duane and Noah are the farmers in the family.)

Duane peered at the closely spaced scribbles that filled many lines. "It's a lot of fine print about farming," he warned Noah, handing him the tablet.

"Yes, I can see that." Noah, being a writer as well as a farmer, took out his own pen. "Here, Melody, I'll write a poem about farming for you." He began to write, pausing now and then to think a little. In a few minutes he showed me his poem before returning the tablet to Melody. He had written:

> Farming is fun, we work in the sun,
> From daylight to dark, all day every day,
> We work and we work for so little pay,
> And when we grumble this is what we say,
> "If I were a carpenter it wouldn't be this way."

"Now, Melody," Noah added, "you make sure your dad sees that." Melody carried the tablet back down the aisle to her carpenter dad.

After a little while she came tripping along the row of seats again. "Here's your letter," she said, flapping her tablet under Noah's nose. Under his rhyme, Melody's dad had scrawled, "You are good."

The little boys were becoming impatient again. They wanted food that didn't come out of our bags crumbled and stale. Wesley stood up on his seat and called toward the back of the bus, "Daddy, will we stop for supper?"

"Ask someone else."

"Hey," Wesley called toward the front of the bus, "will we stop for supper?"

"Ask your daddy."

"But I already did," Wesley cried, sounding frustrated.

"Then go through the bus and ask everyone else."

Soon we would stop for supper somewhere, soon we would sleep, soon we would arrive home. I settled back in my seat to enjoy the ride, the motion of the bus as it hummed west on the highway with the dull rumble of the engine sounding like the contented purr of a great beast. I listened to the scattered bursts of laughter, the swirling of many conversations.

It is good to get out sometimes, to travel on interstate highways and cross state lines and experience a little of the wider world. To see the teeming of much traffic, the thousands of people, the massive buildings and cities on the skyline, the urban sprawl of countless homes, and the vastness of forests and mountains and sky. It's good to learn again how huge the world beyond one's doorstep really is.

But, I thought, coming home is always the best part. There in southern Ohio, in the hilly backcountry of the Appalachian foothills, is home. Home and family and Tuesdays with Mom and my sisters.

The wedding and the trip had been worth every moment of excitement and ruckus and hassle and planning. But now April was over. Spring had begun. And the rest of the year was waiting to be lived.

• • •

"But our God is in the heavens: he hath done whatsoever
he hath pleased."

PSALM 115:3

MAY

Mom's Three-Ring Circus

TUESDAYS AT MOM'S house in May resemble one of those three-ring circuses we used to read about years ago. There are two reasons for this.

It's the peak of the greenhouse season, for one thing, with a steady stream of customers coming and going. And long days of sunshine and warm temperatures mean almost constant watering is needed to keep the plants thriving and healthy.

The second thing that turns May into a farm-based circus is the end of another school term. Suddenly, seven more children show up on Tuesdays, demanding their share of excitement and adventure, and each contributing plenty in the way of noise, confusion, and laughter.

They count the weeks sometimes—"Only four more weeks until I can go along on Tuesdays"; "Only two weeks"—and then at last the end-of-year tests are finished, report cards are distributed, last-day excitements are over, and "Grandma, here we come."

This year Alisha and Carrie were the only girls in school, but there were five boys—Lowell, Dean, Bradley, Tristan, and Travis.

They had been counting the days to go to Mom's house again, slightly older but no less eager to be included in the merry Tuesday air and change of routine.

Alisha, having just graduated from seventh grade, was sitting on the seat beside me, alternately tapping her foot on the floor of the carriage and pushing it against the front. "Come on, Mom. Make Charlotte go faster. She doesn't have to be so slow."

"Oh, calm down," I replied. I was feeling a little out of sorts. "We'll arrive in plenty of time. There's no hurry."

"But I want to be early," Alisha protested.

I didn't reply, because I was feeling unusually blue. It was Cody's first summer to be missing out on Tuesdays at Mom's house, and I was slightly depressed about it. It was hard for him to see us go without him, being still young enough that fishing and playing and roaming around on Grandpa's farm looked more appealing to him than working all day on Noah's produce farm. And yet I knew that he was also old enough that it was time for work to take precedence over play and freedom.

But that didn't make it any easier for me to go without him, and I was wondering when this had happened and why so fast. I had been taking him along to Mom's house for fifteen years now, yet the days had somehow melted away and vanished. I realized just how swiftly the other day when a deep voice rumbled behind me, "Mom?" It brought me up short.

What happened? I asked myself. Why did no one tell me the years would be so short? After all, he's been calling me Mom for a decade and a half now (the first months it sounded more like "Wa wa wa," but I understood anyway), but never before in quite that tone. I'll have to get used to this all over again.

Of course, I consoled myself, it's only Tuesdays that are different now, and he hasn't outgrown any of his teasing yet. Just last Sunday I was busy getting dinner, too busy to notice that the reason he was skulking around the kitchen wasn't only because he was hungry. I finished chopping lettuce for the salad and picked up the ice cube tray to place it in the freezer. In a hurry as usual, I flung open the door of the freezer . . .

"Aahrrgghh!" I said at the top of my lungs.

Matthan's lifelike plastic snake was gliding among the packages of beef patties, with its tail curled near the top of the ice cube trays.

I slammed the door shut and glowered across the room at Cody. He grinned provokingly. I had just made his day. Probably his week.

The years are very short, I thought now, while Charlotte trotted along the narrow gravel road, and this time is short as well. I'd better appreciate these moments, even the ones that annoy, for they will be over too soon. What was that verse somewhere in the Psalms, about days like grass?

"As for man, his days are as grass: as a flower of the field, so he flourisheth. For the wind passeth over it, and it is gone; and the place thereof shall know it no more" (Psalm 103:15-16).

Which would be sad to ponder, except the next verses add, "But the mercy of the Lord is from everlasting to everlasting upon them that fear him, and his righteousness unto children's children; To such as keep his covenant, and to those that remember his commandments to do them."

I needed the reminder. Days pass and childhood vanishes. But there's another world beyond this one where God has prepared changeless perfection for those who love and serve him. Nothing will be sad there.

• • •

At last Charlotte jogged the carriage with Alisha and the rest of us into the lane, around the greenhouses, and up the hill. We'd arrived again.

Piled on the couch inside the door was a heap of shirts and coats. "Take whatever you want," Mom urged us. "The boys here have either outgrown them or don't want them any longer."

We sorted through the pile, choosing shirts that were sizes we needed for our boys to grow into, or coats they could wear next winter. I soon had a stack of both that Cody could wear before long if he kept on growing as fast as he had all year.

"I'll donate what's left to the community yard sale this weekend," Mom added. The yard sale is held at the produce auction building each year, and all proceeds go to help with church and community expenses. "I have some other things to take too, so whatever you don't want of this I'll add to that pile."

I had brought one of my diseased African violets to show Mom its deformed shape. "Would you say this is the work of mites?" I asked, tilting the pot toward her.

Mom took one look at it and seemed a little alarmed. "Keep that thing away from my violets. Something is certainly wrong with it, and it must be mites of one sort or another."

I carried the offending plant out through the back door and dumped it in the field. That should be far enough from Mom's violets, and I wasn't interested in trying to cure it.

"A few of mine have symptoms of a virus," Mom told me when I came back into the house. She removed a few pots from one shelf. "See the half-shaped new leaves, and the spots on them? Both are signs of the African violet virus. I still don't know where they would have picked it up."

· · ·

I returned the fifth Benjie book to the library and was amazed to find a sixth book in the series lying on the table. "Won't Matthan be thrilled?" I remarked. "We just finished reading the last chapter in the final book last night, and he wasn't happy about that. He insisted we're going to start over with the first book and read them all again."

"I just brought that one along today," Emily said. "Tristan had it at home for a while."

I added it to the growing pile of things in my basket. "Anyway, I'm so glad I don't have to start over with Benjie, book one."

Mom was holding David, and when Amanda came she put Ashley in her other arm. "Of course I can hold both babies," Mom said in answer to Amanda's question. But David wasn't sure about this setup. He wore an unmistakable frown and looked as peeved as an eight-month-old baby could. Soon he gave Ashley a gentle smack on the cheek with one hand. Was it deliberate, or was it just happenstance? Ashley looked sober, as if trying to decide.

Mom was trying not to laugh. "I really think David is jealous that I dare hold another baby. Maybe we should get out the walker for him. He may like that better than just sitting here."

I rolled the walker out of the middle room, lifted David off Mom's lap, and slid him into the walker. As I did so, David gave Mom the most accusing look a baby could manage. Then he settled down to grab at the toys dangling along the walker tray.

Janessa sat on Amanda's lap, looking unhappy and whining. "Janessa, what's the matter with you this morning?" I asked.

Amanda looked exasperated. "She's begging to go to JR's to buy candy. Can you believe it?"

"Now, Janessa," Mom said, "you want to play at Grandma's house for a while yet before you go to JR's."

None of the other children had a problem finding something to do. Alisha and the little girls grabbed flashlights and rushed off to the barns. There was a nest of kittens in each one, and Alisha was determined to find and tame them.

The five boys, newly released from school, weren't sure what to do first. They ran off to check on the fishing hole, then they ran back up the hill to set up the croquet game. When that was no longer exciting enough they took turns climbing into the forked branches of the maple tree beside the trampoline and leaping out of it. They hit the trampoline hard and were catapulted back into the air. It's something their uncles did years ago, and now, suddenly, these boys were old enough to try it too.

Matthan and Corey were perched on the slide, practicing auctioneering at full volume and with great joy. But before long we heard loud squalling and roaring; we looked up from what we were doing. "Are some cats fighting?" I asked.

Nathan, who was spending a final week at home before heading back to Alaska, looked up from his newspaper and peered out the window.

"Are they all still in one piece?" Amanda inquired.

"I think so," Nathan grinned. "Corey doesn't look too happy though. He's on the trampoline now, and the others are jumping too high."

"I wish he'd stay off there when the bigger boys are on it," Regina said, going out to lift him off. "He doesn't like bouncing around like that, and he can't jump when they do."

• • •

By now gardens everywhere were bristling with rows of lettuce, and salad was a part of many meals. I dumped the pile I had brought into the sink and began to wash it.

"I picked this in my little greenhouse, and it used to be so easy to wash because it stays clean in there," I explained to Emily, who was helping with salad fixings. "There's no rain to splash mud on it. But now that it's so warm I'm finding aphids again."

Regina came to the sink. "What should I do to help with dinner preparations?" she asked.

"I really don't have any idea at the minute," Mom answered.

"All right, I'll go outside and ramble through the flowers," Regina said. "I'd rather do that anyhow."

"Wait for me," I begged. "We could go after dinner. Right now I have to wash these aphids off the lettuce. I should spray it, I guess, but I'd rather put up with a few bugs."

"Aphids won't hurt anyone," Mom said. "Just before you were born," she told me, "I was laid up with a blood clot in one leg, and your dad brought me a sandwich one day. He'd picked some lettuce in the garden and put it on. I'm sure he'd washed it first, but it was still sprinkled with a few aphids. We had been married for a little less than a year yet, and I suppose I was still wearing my Sunday shoes. I didn't want to complain about it, so I ate those aphids."

"You ate them!" I exclaimed. "No wonder I turned out as I did."

"You mean smart enough to write books?" Emily asked.

"No, I don't think smart is what I mean at all," I protested. "You don't have to be smart to write books." Some days I think foolhardy or crazy or a glutton for punishment more closely describes it.

"Well, these days I would ask to have the aphids washed off," Mom admitted.

• • •

We stretched the table across the kitchen as far as it would go and sorted out several children from the clamoring, pleading throng to be the first ones to eat outside. Wesley, Corey, Janessa, and Luella turned out to be lucky, and the older ones were persuaded to wait for their turn.

I carried cups and the pitcher of water outside to where they had set up the little table. Bits of sunlight coming through the leaves overhead flecked the tabletop, the pint-sized blue chairs, and the children's happy, upturned faces.

Inside, the long table was noisy with conversation and the schoolboys' chatter. "I get rowdy sometimes," Bradley admitted, "but I don't get hyper." He couldn't explain the difference when we asked.

Alisha was speaking to Jerelyn. "Guess what? Mom's next book, the one about Tuesdays, has been accepted."

"We could get into a fight or something here at the table," Lowell suggested with a gleam in his eyes. "Then she would write about that."

"No, no," I protested. "That wouldn't do at all."

"You could call Dean 'Ketchup' in your book," Lowell said. "He likes ketchup so much."

"You could call me Donut," Matthan said. "Or Waffle." He was suggesting his favorite foods.

"Call me Musky," said one of the other boys, remembering the fun he had fishing.

They continued suggesting new names, both for themselves and for each other, and each one became more far-out than the last.

"But I don't want to change your names," I told them at last. "That would be far too much work."

"The people who know us would try to figure out who's who anyway," Emily said, "and those who don't know us won't care."

When dessert was passed, Matthan heaped his plate full of cream cheese dessert, and didn't stop until Alisha intervened. "Mom! Matthan's getting a big pile of dessert."

"That sure sounds like a big sister," Lowell muttered in the direction of his plate.

"Do you know anything about big sisters?" I asked as we moved the dessert away from Matthan. "I sure do," Lowell exclaimed.

"Little sisters aren't any better," Bradley said with a grin. "They sure are sassy too."

"My manners are buried in Knicely's sawmill pile," Matthan remarked to no one in particular.

"I left my manners in Snyder," Makayla confided with disarming sweetness.

• • •

The sun was hot and bright that afternoon as we walked through the rows of irises in the garden. They were in full bloom now, a hundred or more different kinds in every shade and color combination, ready to dig and sell. I admired them in Mom's garden, especially the new varieties with frilly, ruffled petals, but irises are one plant I don't really care for. I like the flowers and their one-of-a-kind perfume, but the bulbs don't do well in my heavy mulching type of gardening.

From the garden we moved on to the greenhouses, where I picked out more plants, including four stalks of okra.

I know the children will never eat okra, so why buy it? There was no good answer, except that it's green and alive and needs a place to grow, and I can find a spot for it somewhere, I'm sure.

I bought more herbs, begonias, and double impatiens, and by then my wallet was empty. In fact, it was registering a minus, but Dad let me have the rest of my plants anyway. "I'll bring the rest of the money along next week," I promised.

I carried my trays of plants over to where my sisters were standing. The children were swarming around the potted strawberry plants, raiding them of all the ripe and partly ripe berries.

"I'm broke," I confessed. "And I still owe Dad four dollars." Then I noticed the pots of succulents Regina was holding. "Come to think of it, I didn't even buy any of those yet. And I have a strawberry planter with holes in the sides that I wanted to fill with succulents."

"Here, would you hold Ashley for me?" Amanda asked, snuggling her baby into my arms. "That should prevent you from buying any more plants."

I was happy to hold Ashley, and I took her to the greenhouse and showed her all the bright and smiling flowers in the long rows. She was not favorably impressed and complained all the while.

"I don't think she likes flowers or greenhouses yet," I told Amanda when she had made her purchases and came to rescue her unhappy baby. When Ashley was back with her mom I slipped off to the far greenhouse and picked out five different succulents for my planter. After all, I reasoned, I could just as well pay for them next week.

When all my plants were finally stowed in the carriage— under the seat, behind the seat, and all over the back seat—I strolled to the porch, where I found Regina with her face near Mom's succulent baskets. "There are two more kinds in the greenhouse I want to buy yet this year," she admitted, "but I'm going to sneak a piece off one of these too."

Jerelyn made a face, and Ida Mae asked, "Do you have to sneak it when Jerelyn isn't looking?"

Regina laughed. "I don't really care whether Jerelyn sees me. I was saying I'll sneak it when Mom isn't looking."

I laughed too, having done the same thing a few times. Of course, if we asked Mom she'd say to go ahead, and we always tell her anyhow.

I pinched a few leaves and small starts off the sides of several new ones. "I tried to start the panda plant like this last year," I commented, pointing to the fuzzy little plant with grayish leaves edged with reddish brown. "But so far it hasn't done a thing. The leaf looks fine, but it doesn't grow a new plant."

"Try laying the leaf on top of the potting soil instead of planting it," Regina advised. "I think it often works better that way. For some reason the leaf grows roots faster just lying on the soil rather than buried in it."

"I'll do that with these," I decided.

"Meanwhile, I can give you a start of some that I have extras of," Regina offered.

"I'd be glad to have them," I said.

Jerelyn, seated on the porch rocker, gave us both a strange look. "Some people are just weird."

Amanda smiled. "I got tired of my succulents last winter. I don't want any more either. But you may enjoy yours."

We sat on the porch where the breeze was cool and the maples cast deep shade. We drank water and iced tea and read letters that Mom had received.

I sat on the glider holding Ashley for so long that Makayla began to be a little worried. "I want to hold Ashley now," she whispered to Amanda.

"Are you afraid Darla will take her along home?" Amanda asked, and Makayla smiled, but she didn't deny it.

"It's been only thirteen years since I cared for a baby girl," I told Makayla. "I think I would still know how." But I let Makayla hold her baby sister, just to reassure her that Ashley still belonged to their family.

"I've invited about twenty or twenty-five people for Sunday dinner a few weeks from now," I told my sisters as we sat there. "Now I need some good ideas for what to fix to eat."

They all wanted to be helpful, and their suggestions were many and varied. Potato wedges. Scalloped potatoes. Ham and cheese poppy seed rolls. Huntington chicken. They decided there should be something with fresh strawberries and vanilla ice cream.

"But when it comes to cooking, even the stores have a conspiracy against me," I complained. "I once bought ice cream to serve to guests that turned out to be sandy, gritty, and the worst ice cream I ever tasted."

Instead of sympathizing, they found my food tribulations a source of amusement. And, come to think of it, they are funny. Just not until a long time later.

• • •

Another Tuesday morning found Alisha, Matthan, and I whizzing downhill on our bikes. It was exhilarating, except that Matthan was going too fast for my comfort. "Slow down, Matthan," I called after him. "Slow down!"

It was with relief that I got him down the hill and in the lane to Mom's house. Once there, he and Corey ran to the barn with Alisha and the other little girls. They had discovered all the new kittens in the haymow, were giving them names, and this morning were bringing them food in hopes of teaching them how to eat.

After the kittens were all properly greeted, Jerelyn and Alisha biked to JR's General Store to buy Dutch Gel for Mom. "I'd like to can strawberry jelly today," Mom explained, also giving them money to buy some soda pop. "And the jelly won't thicken if the Dutch Gel isn't fresh."

"So that's what is wrong with my strawberry jelly," I said. "The Dutch Gel I used is several years old, and my jelly is only slightly thicker than water."

"It seems to work that way," Mom agreed. "It's best to buy fresh Dutch Gel every year."

We exchanged jelly-making stories while we sorted out our things, and the boys disappeared to the water hole with their fishing gear. Matthan tagged after them in search of some excitement.

When the girls came back from the store they distributed the pop, and even carried cans down the lane for the fishermen, who then decided to also come up to the house. Matthan came indoors wearing a disgruntled expression. He had found more excitement than he had bargained for.

"My clothes are wet," he grumbled. "Feel my shirt. The boys were splashing water around, and all over us."

"That's what happens when you run along with the big boys," I told him. "Why don't you stay at the house now and play with Wesley and Corey?"

• • •

The morning dew dried from the grass, and we hauled out both lawn mowers, to start on the endless job of cutting grass. The schoolboys took turns, and between turns they lay on their backs on the trampoline reading books from the library while high above them in the branches of the silver maple a concerned mother oriole scolded because they were too close to her nest.

I walked past them on the way to the house and almost wished I could join them, they looked so carefree. The girls were idling on the swings, the younger children were at play in the cool shade of the maples, and at the moment everything was peaceful. It was a minute to appreciate while it lasted.

We heated chicken strips in the oven, washed and chopped lettuce, opened packages of shredded cheese, and found bottles of ranch dressing. Then we layered it all on tortilla wraps and rolled them up for our dinner.

We set the table for twenty-four people and carried things outside on the lawn for Carrie, KellyAnn, Melody, and Matthan, who were the lucky ones today. They were a lively foursome. Matthan and his chair fell over backward, and the girls giggled, so he did it again. The harder the girls giggled the more often his chair fell over. "Doesn't Matthan mind that he's the only boy with three girls?" Ida Mae asked, concerned.

"Oh, no, he doesn't mind," I sighed. "The more the girls laugh at him, the sillier he acts, and the sillier he acts, the more they laugh."

"What's happening in your life that's exciting?" I asked Christopher when he came in for dinner. "I need something to write about, and your life is probably more interesting than all of ours put together."

Christopher just grinned and did not reply.

"It's May," Mom pointed out. "Of course there's nothing interesting going on. Our lives just revolve around the greenhouses."

When dinner was over Emily tackled the huge stack of dishes. "I'll be finished sometime before tomorrow," she remarked with a little sigh as we stored away the extra leaves for the table and pushed it back into its usual place.

Outside on the porch two cardboard boxes with assorted cans and bottles stood on the white wrought iron table. "If any of you want some of these fertilizers or organic garden sprays, help yourself," Mom said after we finally finished with the dishes and were ready to prop up our feet on chairs on the porch. "I don't want them."

I scanned the labels. Fungicide, organic fertilizers, hot pepper sprays, oil sprays, organic insecticide. "Where did you get this stuff?"

"A lady dropped it off at the greenhouse last week. She said I could have it. I took out a few bottles, but I won't use all of that."

We browsed through the boxes. Regina found some rooting formula and a fungicide for her succulents. Emily discovered some of the sprays they used for their fruit trees, Amanda sorted out several organic fertilizer sprays that were ready to use, and I found plenty to drag along home as well.

Regina had brought some of her tea concentrate, and we mixed it up and took glasses of it to the porch. This concentrate is handy to have and simple to make.

TEA CONCENTRATE

4 cups water
2 cups sugar
2 cups tightly packed tea leaves

In a large saucepan, bring water and sugar to a boil and boil for 5 minutes. (Less sugar can be used.) Add tea leaves; let the mixture stand 6 or 7 hours, or overnight. Use 1 cup concentrate to 2 quarts water, or to taste. Freeze for winter use, or refrigerate to use as needed. It tastes like fresh tea.

When I came outside with my glass of tea, I found Regina at the corner of the porch, scrutinizing the potted succulents once again.

"Are there any new ones?" I called to her as I sank into a chair.

"Just what was here the last time I looked," Regina said with a laugh.

Mom sat down on the rocker nearby. "I couldn't find anything new at the garden centers to get excited about this year."

The children, meanwhile, were getting excited about choosing flowers. Matthan wanted a pack of pink dianthus; Melody had potted plants with long fuzzy red flowers like elongated caterpillars. "We're going to make hanging baskets with them," she explained, showing me what she had chosen. Makayla was on her way past my chair "driving" Luella, who was her horse, with a jump rope for the reins. "I picked some too," she said with a little smile.

"What did you pick?" I asked.

"Ohhh, it had colorful leaves," she replied, thinking hard.

"Coleus?" I guessed.

"Yes, I picked a coleus." She pointed at Matthan's dianthus. "And I got some like that too."

A black plastic mailbox and post were lying on the glider, and Melody and Makayla pulled open the lid to peer inside. "Such a big mailbox," Melody exclaimed. "I could probably crawl into it." She clambered up over the arm of the glider and tried to get inside the mailbox. "Only one leg fits in, though," she announced.

Makayla was watching her. "I would probably fit inside."

"Don't break my new mailbox," Mom called to Melody.

"Aren't you afraid someone will come along and smash it after you put it up at the end of the lane?" Emily asked. Such vandalism has been only too common in our rural area.

"Our old one hasn't been bothered for quite a few years now," Mom replied, "and it's so worn out the mail gets wet every time it rains. So we'll risk it. The salesperson at Lowe's assured me that this kind is hard to smash."

Several minutes later Matthan ran past the glider and yanked open the lid of the mailbox. In another second he was up on the glider and trying to get into it.

"Matthan," I exclaimed. "Grandma doesn't want you in there."

"I don't want it broken before I even put it up," Mom explained as Matthan climbed back out. "Why do you suppose the children all want to get into it?" she wondered.

No one knew. Why did they feel a need to climb into an empty mailbox, or dabble in mud puddles, or catch frogs to figure out how they jump, or any of the 101 things children do at play?

Carrie was hovering around the table, peering curiously at my notebook. "What can I write about you, Carrie?" I asked.

Carrie has big brown eyes that positively sparkle, and they were sparkling now. "Nothing," she said quickly, with a smile that made dimples appear on her cheeks.

"Oh, you can read now," I remembered. "No wonder you like to peep at my notebook. I keep forgetting that you have already finished second grade." Not only my children, but all the others also were growing up almost faster than I could believe.

"When is Noah's campout this year?" Emily asked, reminding me that I had also been wondering.

Regina was the only one who knew. "Noah told Duane they've planned it for the first weekend in July, like usual," she told us. Noah's campout at his farm is an annual family event the children often begin to anticipate before school has even ended for the summer. "The children would be so disappointed if we had to miss it for some reason."

Matthan and Melody traded bikes and were trying to ride each other's, but it wasn't working too well because Matthan's bike was almost too big for Melody. They were still struggling along when it was nearly time to go home. Mom brought a container with assorted candies to the porch. Bikes and other toys were dropped as the children ran to help themselves. "Just one handful," Mom cautioned. "I want everyone to be able to have some."

She passed it to us next, knowing that even moms like candy occasionally. "No, thanks," Ida Mae said.

"Don't hold candy in front of her," Emily added.

"Oh sorry!" Mom exclaimed. "I wasn't thinking."

"That's all right." Ida Mae sighed. "At least it seems like there's an end in sight now."

"You could start putting some candy in a bag and saving it until after the baby is born," Amanda suggested, only half teasing. "Or even keep a pan of dessert in the freezer to eat later."

"The year Melody was born I did save some Christmas cookies and kept them in the freezer to eat later on," Ida Mae admitted. "I doubt I'll start saving candy or desserts, though."

The boys were fishing at the water hole again, and Melody and Carrie ran down the lane to call them, luring them up to the house with the promise of Grandma's candy. Even so, they came reluctantly and with complaints. In their opinion, another Tuesday could not already be over.

When Bradley appeared on the porch he was running a hand over his arm. "Mom! A tick."

"Take it to the bathroom and flush it," Ida Mae said, unwilling to deal with it.

"I'll just pull it apart instead," Bradley decided, and did so; and another Tuesday ended on this note, with laughter and the last of chatter as we gathered up our children and belongings and prepared to depart.

• • •

"Teach me thy way, O Lord; I will walk in thy truth."

PSALM 86:11

JUNE

Zucchini Kayaks, Spatula Showers, and Silicone Cupcake "Papers"

THE FIRST TUESDAY in June I had an errand that would delay my arrival at Mom's house by perhaps fifteen minutes. "Drop me off at the lane," Alisha requested, not wanting to miss a minute of her day. "I'll walk the rest of the way."

"I'll walk too," Matthan decided, so I brought Charlotte to a halt at the edge of the driveway. The children leaped from the carriage and ran along the lane without a backward glance. It was Tuesday and they were at Grandpa's farm, and Mom didn't count as much as finding some cousins and playmates.

When I returned a brief quarter of an hour later, I saw they hadn't even made it to the house. Christopher was cutting zucchini in the field beside the lane, and Regina and her boys were helping him finish. Along the rows, white buckets brimming with zucchini waited to be hauled to the packing shed. Alisha and Matthan were wading through the rows of knee-high plants and reaching past the scratchy zucchini leaves to the center of the stalk to cut off the ones ready to pick.

I made my way to the house with my basket and my contribution to the noon meal. Before long Regina and Alisha came to the house too, and the little girls all skipped off to the barn with Alisha. They wanted to check on the kittens, to see how much they had grown in a week and which one had been given away to a new home, and to play with the ones that were left.

We sorted out the books and magazines to return and exchange, plopped casseroles and desserts and cookies on the counter for dinner, and decided what we still needed to complete the meal, in between talking about all the ordinary but nevertheless interesting details of our daily lives.

Quite a while later the door banged behind Melody as she came inside. "Is Matthan here?"

"Matthan?" I looked around the kitchen. "No, he's not. I don't know where he is."

"I wanted to play with him," Melody explained, "but I can't find him."

I stepped outside on the porch and scanned the swings, slide, and trampoline. The girls had left the kittens in the barn and were playing in the yard. Wesley was with them, but Matthan and Corey were nowhere to be seen. "I'll go look for him, Melody," I said. "It's strange that he's not around anywhere."

Melody trotted beside me as we walked down the lane to check the boys' favorite spot first. The fishing hole was deserted and silent, except for the low trickling hum of water splashing from the culvert. We started back up the lane.

"Let's check the zucchini field," I suggested next, and we followed the dusty lane to where it wandered behind the barn. Melody chattered as we strolled, and I learned several new ways of looking at old things.

We crossed the old wooden bridge over the creek and rounded the corner of the fencerow. A little knot of boys was crouched near the center of the zucchini field, dark heads bent over something that was absorbing their wholehearted interest.

Melody skipped barefooted through the rows to join them, and they all looked up at our approach. Matthan and Corey were in the group, and they all looked happy. "We're making boats," they explained.

"And kayaks," Dean said, holding up an overgrown zucchini with its center hollowed out.

"And canoes," Tristan added, digging his pocketknife into another huge zucchini.

"Here's my boat," Matthan said, waving his zucchini-craft over his head.

A pile of zucchini too large to sell, a couple of pocketknives, and boys eager to practice their carving skills—no wonder they were still in the zucchini field.

Matthan and Corey decided to go to the house with Melody and me, and the three of them chased me up the lane, making a game of trying to catch me.

"You can be our slave," Melody explained, for Ida Mae had just finished reading a book about the Underground Railroad to her children for their bedtime story. "We'll be the people that try to catch you." I suspect they weren't the first children to make a game out of sad, serious history.

They chased after me, laughing as I dodged this way and that. But there were three of them and they were fleet of foot and more used to running than I was. Before long I let them catch me and escort me to the house.

When the older boys came to the house shortly after us and dumped their load of zucchini boats, kayaks, and canoes on the ground beneath the trees, Wesley eyed them with displeasure. "I want some big zucchini too," he whined, marching into the house to yank on Emily's apron. "Mom, please come with me to the field. I want to make boats too."

"Matthan would probably go with you," I told Wesley.

"I'll go with you too," Melody offered. "I know where the big zucchini are."

"I want to go too," KellyAnn said.

Makayla began to squirm on the chair where she was perched while Amanda combed her hair. "I want to go along," she begged.

"Can you wait a little bit longer?" Amanda asked the children. "I'm almost done with Makayla's braids, and she would really like to go with you."

They danced around impatiently, and by the time Makayla's hair was braided, Matthan and Wesley were at the bottom of the hill, prancing in circles, but still waiting. Then they all skipped down the long field lane in the sunshine.

They returned a while later, trudging uphill much more slowly, loaded down with all the large zucchini they could carry. "I wonder why there are so many large ones," Mom remarked. "It's the beginning of the season and usually they don't get so big until later."

"The zucchini were ready for a few days before the men realized they should be picked," Regina explained. "That's why there were so many that had to be discarded this morning."

Corey came puffing indoors, his face flushed. "They were heavy," he said, having just dragged uphill a few of the biggest ones.

Wesley didn't want to leave his outside. He stood outside the door hollering, "Mom! Open the door. Mom, I have a zucchini load." Five enormous ones were falling out of his arms when Emily opened the door.

"Who put a spatula in here?" Mom asked as we began making dinner. She pointed to the crock in the corner of the sink, from which sprouted an assortment of kitchen utensils.

Ida Mae looked puzzled. "Isn't that where it belongs?" Mom's dishes have a way of turning up in funny places after we wash them on Tuesdays, but the utensils were straightforward. We stuck all of them into that crock.

"No, I mean someone put a new spatula in here and threw an old one away." Mom watched Amanda's face. She knew that was what we had done with her old vegetable peeler when we got tired of using it. "I thought it might have been Amanda."

Instead it was Emily who looked guilty. "I put the new spatula in there. But just because I found an extra one in a box of other sale items, and I didn't need it."

"You could actually use a few more new ones," Amanda remarked, for Mom's cracked and nicked spatulas have elicited comments from us more than once. "We could put a 'spatula shower' in *Die Botschaft* for you," she added. The weekly newspaper for Amish and Old Order Mennonite communities often had several columns dedicated to "showers" asking for cards or letters or other things for people who had been ill or who otherwise needed encouragement.

"A 'high-quality' spatula shower," Emily said, laughing. "Then we'll throw away all these old ones."

Mom shook her head. She knew we were teasing.

"Actually, old and cracked spatulas can poison you," Amanda added. "I've read that chemicals or something will leach from the plastic after it's cracked."

"Then I guess these would have poisoned us long ago," Mom replied, unalarmed.

Carrie was concerned about the sore on the mother cat's foot. "It's hurting her," she worried. "She's limping."

"We may have to put ointment on it and wrap up her foot until it heals," Mom said. "But right now, why don't you just make sure that she and her kittens have enough food."

Carrie was happy to do that, but there was one thing she wanted even more, which was why she was tagging after Regina. "Mom, the kittens are older now. I could take one home. Please, may I have one?"

Jerelyn shook her head. "We already have a dog, Carrie. We don't want a cat too."

"But I'm not asking you." Carrie continued to follow Regina. "Please, Mom, may I have a kitten?"

Regina sighed. "You'll have to ask Daddy. He can decide."

There were many things to talk about as we worked together to put dinner on the table. Refrigerators were working harder now, in the summer heat, and we discussed at length which model was best and why and if it would be better to have several small ones instead of a single large one. It's amazing how many opinions there can be about refrigerators.

We mentioned things from Sunday's sermon, still remembered and appreciated, and touched briefly on the horse sale a few of us had attended on Saturday, wondering why the price for a good horse remained so high.

And then, of most interest, there was baby Conrad, born six weeks early to Noah and Christine. He was still in the hospital in Cincinnati because his birth weight was five pounds ten ounces. He was doing well and would surely be able to come home soon. Perhaps this week. None of us had yet seen this newest, tiniest member of the family. It was important to meet him as soon as possible, to decide whether he favored Noah or Christine, or both. And how was twenty-two-month-old Rosalyn adjusting, and was Conrad contented and good, and did he sleep well at night?

"I suppose the campout will be rescheduled for later in the summer," someone said. The children would be disappointed, but both mother and baby would certainly appreciate more time to rest before we all descended upon their farm for a campout.

It was growing cloudy. Before long, raindrops started a muffled waltz on the roof. I removed the flowerpots that were on the porch table and readied it for the children who would eat outside at noon. But none of them seemed concerned about getting wet. Instead, they came in out of the drizzle reluctantly, pleading to be allowed to jump on the trampoline in the rain.

Since the trampoline was partly sheltered by overhanging maple branches, and the rain, little more than a drizzle, had not yet penetrated the heavy leaf canopy, they received permission. Soon a mob of screeching boys and girls was bouncing up and down, and the faster the rain fell, the higher they jumped, and the better they liked it.

Domineering moms that we were, we called them all indoors before the rain turned into a downpour, ignoring the inevitable protests that it really wasn't wet. We settled everyone at the tables, the older children at the long one indoors, and the smallest children at the table on the porch.

The older boys washed their hands noisily, laughing about an ongoing joke they were having, one that included the possibility of having nothing on their plates to eat except rotten tomatoes and potato bugs.

"You won't find any potato bugs," Mom told them. "I'm not even finding any on my potatoes this year," she added, sounding pleased. "It must not be a good year for bugs."

"Grandma," Lowell said, "we're picking them all off and using them as bait when we go fishing."

"Well!" Mom exclaimed. "So that's why I haven't seen any potato bugs this year."

"They make good bait," the boys agreed.

"I must tell Arlie about this," Mom said. "We were just telling each other how nice it is not to have any bugs eating the potato plants this year."

"Do you go over the road and pick hers too?" Dad asked the boys.

"Oh, no, Grandpa," they assured him. "We're just using yours for our bait."

We usually crowd a long line of children onto the bench behind the table, and this keeps one or more of us busy hopping up to help them pass the food or fill their plates.

"We really should put a mom between the children every so often," Amanda suggested. "It would make it all a little easier."

KellyAnn leaned forward. "But not you beside me," she called up the table.

"Then you can sit beside me," Emily told KellyAnn, "and I can make sure you behave."

"I didn't really mean it would be to keep you in order," Amanda explained to KellyAnn. "I just thought it would make it easier to help you all with the dishes full of food."

The schoolboys were discussing the summer task of lawn mowing, and they all agreed they weren't fond of it. "Sometimes Travis takes a turn too," Tristan said. "Then the lines get very wiggly because he likes to chase after the bees in the grass with the mower."

"Sometimes I do that too," Bradley admitted.

"But Travis can't mow a lot of grass yet," Tristan added. "Especially not on the hill."

"Sometimes Melody thinks she should be able to help mow the grass," Bradley complained. "That really slows me up."

I looked at the pile of dishes and realized it was my turn to wash them. "Boys," I said, "if you want to do the dishes I could take a turn mowing grass. I sort of enjoy it."

"No, no, no!" Dean and Tristan and Bradley replied in almost the same voice and tone of horror. "Mowing lawn is still much better than washing dishes."

"I enjoy mowing grass too," Mom said. "It's not such a bad job."

• • •

The silicone cupcake papers turned up at dinner again. Amanda had brought muffins; about half of them were blueberry and half of them were banana. "Did you remember that I have to wash dishes today, and do this on purpose?" I asked Amanda, trying to sound annoyed.

After all, the stacks of dishes resembled skyscrapers and now I had to wash the cupcake papers too.

"I'm sure I must have," Amanda said, laughing. "No, I'm just teasing you." She began gathering them together, with Ashley in one arm, who was complaining like the sleepy baby she was. "You don't have to wash them," Amanda said. "I'll take them along home and scrub them tonight with my supper dishes."

She left the stack at the bottom of the table and went to rock Ashley to sleep for her nap.

I plowed my way through the dishes. "And I really do intend to wash those cupcake papers too," I said to Emily, who was drying. "I'll just sneak them into the sink bowl when Amanda isn't looking."

It was a big stack of cupcake papers, and they really were tiresome to wash, but I managed. "And now I will have to dry them," Emily sighed when they appeared in the drainer.

Ashley soon slept, and Amanda came back to the kitchen just as we were finishing. "Did you really wash and dry those things? I was serious when I said I'd do it at home." She laughed. "But at least now I get to sew my new dress instead."

• • •

There was a line of six children running downhill hand in hand. Wesley, Corey, Melody, Luella, Makayla, and Janessa were going to the barn to play with the kittens.

We also headed downhill after the dishes were done and the rain was over, but our destination was the greenhouse. Immediately after Memorial Day, prices are reduced and we get everything we still want for free, this being a fringe benefit of being the daughters of the owners.

The tables in the greenhouses were starting to appear empty and picked over, but there were still quite a few plants left. We filled trays with annuals, coleus, vines for hanging baskets, and geraniums. Walking down one aisle, I noticed that all but one lone pot of my elephant ears had sold, and I hoped that one would sell soon. I didn't want to plant it at home.

A single line of huge fern baskets still dangled from the top of the greenhouse. "I wonder if I want any ferns to babysit this year," Emily said, almost to herself.

"I had some last year," I said, "but I think I'll skip it this time." Sometimes we would take a few of the leftover ferns home to keep on our porches over the summer. They were what Dad would keep for stock for the following year, so we always brought them back to the greenhouse again just before the first frost in October. We jokingly called it babysitting ferns for Dad.

I liked the potted Boston ferns, but the carriage was filling up fast and I still wanted some New Guinea impatiens and gerbera daisies. Besides, I had enough plants to take care of over the summer, potted and otherwise. I would show great restraint and willpower this year and refrain from hauling home any ferns.

Up the middle aisle of the greenhouse came Matthan and Wesley, their faces flushed and sweaty. With one hand they were each dragging an empty horse feed bag that they had unearthed in the barn. In their other hand they clutched enormous bunches of the tall yellow primroses that had been growing beside the barn. The flowers had been yanked out by the roots and were already limp.

Emily and I burst out laughing. "Whatever are we teaching you boys?" Emily inquired.

That question could be taken two ways, I decided. Either that all of Mom's flowers and plants are up for grabs or that we're not teaching them enough about respecting other people's property.

"Oh, we left some there for Grandma too," Matthan and Wesley assured us.

When we finally finished selecting the plants we still wanted, we took turns mowing some of the lawn, switching off with Jerelyn and Alisha, and then sitting on the front porch where the breeze was cooler. The boys set up the croquet game in the shade, but the little girls were still busy imitating their mothers.

Janessa pattered uphill first, a dark-eyed little girl carrying a pretty pink basket by its white handle, pink petunias trailing over the sides. Then came KellyAnn and Melody; both of them were hiding their hands behind their backs and smiling.

"May we have these?" Melody asked, and both girls pulled pots of succulents from behind their backs to flourish in front of their moms' eyes.

Ida Mae made a face. "I just looked at the succulents when I was in the greenhouse and thought, I'm so glad I never started growing any of those. Now here it comes."

"Listen, girls," Mom said. "Those succulents are more like houseplants. Why don't you take them back to the greenhouse and trade them for something like impatiens or petunias? Something that you can plant in a flower bed and it will grow for you."

The girls did so. And Carrie came up from the barns, her eyes glowing, to announce that she had chosen a kitten to take along home, her daddy having given his permission. Those big eyes would be hard for anyone to resist when they were pleading. Little girls, kittens, and summer days go together like graham crackers, marshmallows, and chocolate.

Then Melody came running uphill. "Mom, Carrie's taking a kitten along home and I want one too."

Ida Mae looked a little tired. "Melody, you know we just got a new puppy for you and Bradley. A German shepherd puppy. He's so rough I don't think he would mix very well with a kitten."

Melody burst into tears. "But we have a haymow in the barn and we could keep the kitten penned up in it."

"She wouldn't stay there all the time," Ida Mae tried to explain. "I'm afraid Twig would kill her as soon as she got out. And remember, you have a miniature horse to play with this summer too."

"Tell us about your little horse, Melody," we said, and her tears were soon forgotten as she told us about Lucy, her miniature horse. The puppy and the little horse would be just as good as a kitten for playmates during the long warm days.

"I simply don't think I can deal with a kitten yet too," Ida Mae sighed after Melody had run off to play again, and we all knew exactly what she meant. Because while the children thrive on the momentary excitement and the fun of having a new pet, all too often it's the mom who gets to take care of the animals after the newness wears off. Or, at the very least, it's the mom who has to make sure the children remember to take care of the pets.

Regina was gathering up her things to go home. "And now I still need Corey's shoes. He left them here last week. Did you find them, Mom?"

"Yes, I did. I put them here on the table."

We all looked at the table. It was empty of shoes.

"Oh," I said sheepishly, "I put those shoes out in the carriage with some other stuff. I thought they were Matthan's."

Regina gave me a strange look. "Well, they used to be Matthan's. You gave them to me for Corey when Matthan outgrew them."

I shook my head. "No wonder I thought I was supposed to take them along home. They looked so familiar." I dashed off to the carriage and rummaged through my things, trying to find where I had put Corey's shoes.

Ida Mae carried an armload of her things to the bike cart. Then she piled everything on the ground beside it and started tossing out zucchini.

"Would you believe it? There are nine zucchini almost as big as baseball bats in my cart. I guess Melody thinks I'm going to haul them home for her."

• • •

Another Tuesday morning rolled around, and I was in my usual packing-up rush. Cody was moseying around, getting ready to leave for Noah's farm, Alisha's hair needed to be combed and braided, and Matthan was lying on the recliner in his pajamas, having just come downstairs. I shoved a cake into the oven to bake and prepared to water the houseplants.

"Mom, every time I look around Matthan is staring at me," Cody said. He sounded irritated as he slipped on his shoes.

"Maybe he's thinking, 'There is my wonderful big brother I love so much,'" I suggested.

A long, loud sigh was my only answer. Then Cody's footsteps clattered down the basement stairs, and soon afterward the outside door closed behind his bike. He was on his way.

I dragged a comb through Alisha's thick hair and started braiding. "Ouch, Mom! Slow down."

"Oh sorry. I'm trying to hurry. I still have to get the milk ready for your cats when I'm finished here." At least milk wasn't a problem at the moment. Cookie the cow was producing all we needed and all the cats could possibly drink.

By the time the cake had baked and the flowers were watered, Matthan was still in his pajamas. I was getting ready to scribble a quick note to friends in Pennsylvania. In less than two weeks we wanted to visit them, and I should let them know about our plans. I didn't have a number to call them, so a short letter would have to suffice.

Mentioning that we would be lodging with people who were strangers to them reminded the children that they had several big concerns about the whole deal. "Do they have any children?" they asked anxiously. "How old are they?" And then—"May I just stay at home?"

I started the letter and wrote a sentence or two between bites of yogurt for my breakfast. Matthan interrupted me first. He was in the bathroom hollering, "Mom! Mom!"

I grabbed his clothes from where I had laid them on the recliner and carried them down the hall to the bathroom. While I was there I remembered several items I needed to add to my shopping list. When you get to the store only two or three times a month, you learn to keep detailed lists, and they grow long.

I got back to my letter at last. I scribbled a few more sentences. This would have to do. I hoped it would make sense when it arrived at its destination.

At ten after eight I took a final glance around the house and dashed out the door to where Alisha and Matthan waited with our bikes. We loaded up the things for Mom's house and got on our bikes at last. Then I remembered! It was eight twelve when

I ran back inside. I had left my letter lying on the table. When the mailbox is almost a mile away through the woods, forgotten letters become a major deal.

On our way at last, I sighed. You really have to be a mother and a homemaker, I thought, to understand how a six-mile bike ride through woods and along back roads can be both desirable and looked forward to as peaceful.

Matthan biked along beside me, filling the still morning air with his chatter. I listened with half of one ear to tales about cowbirds shaped like tiny cows with a wing on each side, a baby duck that had died because it had gotten wet (was that actually the real reason, I wondered), and the many frogs at the pond: green frogs, leopard frogs, bullfrogs.

Traffic is usually light in the morning, and today it was almost nonexistent. We met one large truck, and the driver waved and smiled.

Matthan waved back. "That was a friendly truck driver," he said.

"Yes," I agreed. "Yes, that's so. But you do remember that you must never accept a ride with someone, even if they're friendly, don't you?"

"Oh, I remember," Matthan said.

"Or take candy, or anything like that, from someone," I persisted.

"I know that," Matthan said, sounding bored.

I pedaled on, reflecting that it was a shame that in today's world we learned so soon to be distrustful and suspicious of even a smile and a wave. I wanted to think the best of people, but usually, especially where my children were concerned, I found myself more wary than trustful. I didn't consider myself a fearful person, and I was not afraid to bike these roads, but I knew that bad things happen, and I preferred to be careful. I liked to remind myself that I didn't need to be afraid, "because greater is he that is in you, than he that is in the world" (1 John 4:4), and I trusted God to take care of us through whatever he allowed to touch our lives, both the good and the bad.

But there is still that innate caution, that unwillingness to take anyone at their word, that wariness that is a by-product of hearing and reading too much of man's inhumanity to man.

• • •

Traffic remained light. Just as we turned in the lane at the farm, a car swooped over the slight hill ahead of us, making it three vehicles that we had met in those six miles and the thirty-five to forty minutes it took us to bike that far.

The boys were already playing at the water hole beside the lane, but they scrambled up the bank to show us the toy snake Tristan had brought. It was made of tiny wooden links all fastened together in a way to form a serpent that twisted in a lifelike manner and made tiny clicking noises that one could imagine sounded like a rattlesnake.

"Ugh, that's awful," I exclaimed. "Why do boys seem to like those frightful toys?"

Bradley dug a small piece of flint out of his shirt pocket. "If you want something to write about you could write about this." The oddly shaped flint lay in his palm. "See, it looks like a bird." At least it wasn't shaped like a snake, and for that I was grateful.

I had brought several books to share with my sisters, just in case they were looking for something to read. *Prayers for a Simpler Life*, by Faith Sommers, was the first one.

"I went to Faith View Books when we were in Holmes County the other week, especially to buy that book," I told them. When you love books as I do, a new one is always special, but it's even more special when the author is a friend and fellow writer. "Then I also found this one." I held up *Plain Choice*, by Sherry Gore. "Of course I had to have this one too." I'd had some contact with Sherry Gore a few years ago, and *Plain Choice* detailed her journey from a California party girl to a woman who had chosen to serve God as a member of an Anabaptist church. It was a thought-provoking read, and one that reminded everyone, no matter who or where they were, that serving God is a choice and that a commitment to him is to be kept for the rest of one's lifetime.

The last one I'd brought wasn't new. I had found it at a secondhand shop, and enjoyed it enough to want to share it. It was called *Just Hand Over the Chocolate and No One Will Get Hurt*, by Karen Scalf Linamen. It was full of down-to-earth inspiration, lighthearted humor, and chocolate, three of my favorite things. Laughter is a necessary part of life for me. I love the Bible verse "A merry heart doeth good like a medicine" (Proverbs 17:22), and it works wonders as stress relief.

• • •

"I picked three five-gallon buckets of peas from my garden," Ida Mae was saying. "So far I've put seventeen bags in the freezer."

"I'm also picking peas now," I said. "I'm not getting that much, though. Mine never seem to do well."

"I plant Green Arrow," Ida Mae said. "That kind usually does well. They have such nice, long pods."

"Mine have powdery mildew so badly," Emily remarked. "Even the pods are white. They're a mess to pick and shell."

"So do mine," I sighed. "I didn't stake them, and now the stalks are so thick and have fallen over. This warm weather made them look so ugly and diseased."

A straggling heap of long green fleshy tubers with a cluster of small onions on one end was lying on the counter. "Here are some of those walking onions," Mom told Emily. "Do Tristan and Travis still want some? I saved these for them if they do."

"I'm sure they'd like to plant some." Emily took the onions gingerly. "I guess we can stick them in somewhere."

Matthan walked in a circle around her, studying the odd clusters. "I want some of those too," he said.

"They can share with you." Emily separated a long stem from the pile and held it out to him. Four small onions grew in a cluster on the end of it.

"But, Matthan, where will you plant it?" I thought about my crowded and overflowing gardens. "I wish you would let Tristan and Travis keep their onions."

But Matthan was sure this was just what he had been wanting all year, so I sighed and said, "I suppose we can put them somewhere. Do they need a lot of space?"

"They can wander over a lot of ground," Mom admitted. "The stems grow top-heavy and fall over, and each little onion on the end begins to grow. Then those stems topple over, and so on. That's why they're called walking onions."

"Edible?" I asked, tucking Matthan's start of the plant into the basket with my other things.

"Oh, I don't think so. I just grow them as an ornamental."

In one outside corner of the porch roof a tiny house wren was ducking in and out of a birdhouse, feeding her noisy babies.

Their cheeping and twittering became positively frenetic each time she appeared with another insect.

Matthan appeared on the porch nearby and held a long earthworm up to the window screen. It dangled, wiggling, from his dirty fingers.

Makayla wrinkled her nose. "What is that?"

I turned to look. "A worm. I wonder where he found it." Matthan climbed up over the glider and perched on the back, arm outstretched toward the birdhouse where the little wrens nestled. They were silent, crouched in the dark cavity.

"Don't get too close, Matthan," I warned him. "And anyway, that worm is too big for the baby birds. They couldn't swallow it."

"Be careful you don't scare them and make them jump out," Mom added.

Wesley and Melody joined Matthan on the glider with a clamor. "What is it? What are you doing? Will they eat it? Can we see?"

"You had better all come away from the birdhouse," I advised the three would-be mother wrens. "Grandma doesn't want you to frighten her birds."

Wesley and Melody jumped to the porch. Matthan balanced on the wobbling glider and reached for a clothespin clipped on the line at the edge of the porch. When he jumped off the glider moments later, the worm remained behind, dangling from the clothesline.

"Maybe the mama wren will find that," someone called to him through the screen.

KellyAnn crossed the porch, pushing a doll stroller. Luella was riding in it. It was a tight fit, but they both looked happy.

• • •

We began peeling potatoes to make German pizza for dinner. "The men around here would rather have a real pizza, so I seldom make this anymore," Mom said. "But it's a simple casserole for today."

GERMAN PIZZA

1 pound ground beef
½ medium onion, chopped
½ green bell pepper, diced
1½ teaspoon salt, divided
½ teaspoon pepper
2 tablespoons butter
6 medium potatoes, peeled and shredded
3 eggs, beaten
⅓ cup milk
2 cups shredded cheddar or mozzarella cheese

In a skillet over medium heat, brown beef with onion, bell pepper, ½ teaspoon salt, and pepper. Remove mixture from skillet, drain fat. Reduce heat to low, add butter to skillet. When butter is melted, spread potatoes over butter and sprinkle with remaining 1 teaspoon salt. Top with beef mixture. Separately, combine eggs and milk; pour over meat and potatoes. Cook, uncovered, until potatoes are tender, about 30 minutes. Top with cheese. Cover, and heat until cheese is melted. Cut into wedges and serve.

As we browned the meat, prepped the potatoes, and grated cheese, Mom came indoors from taking out the potato peelings, and she was laughing. "I found a few busy little farmers in the watermelon field behind the house," she said. It turned out that Matthan, Corey, Wesley, and Makayla had discovered all the miniature watermelons growing in those long rows of plastic that stretched through the field. "They were yanking hard at some of those little watermelons," Mom said, "but I don't think they had pulled any off the vines yet."

We went to peer out the window. "They're all on the trampoline now," Emily said.

"Yes, I told them to go jump awhile," Mom said. "I thought it would be best if they forgot about those little watermelons."

While the casserole baked we set the long table in the kitchen. I went outside and removed the potted flowers from the porch table again and set it for the children who would have a turn eating outside. I was at the sink filling the pitcher with water when Melody flounced indoors. "Who set the table on the porch?" she demanded. "I wanted to eat at the little table again."

"Sorry, Melody," I called, trying not to laugh. "I didn't know you would disapprove."

"Surely it doesn't matter where you eat," Ida Mae said reasonably. "The food will taste the same."

"But I wanted to eat out on the grass," Melody wailed, close to tears.

"You go ahead and take your little table out under the trees," I said. "I didn't know that was what you wanted."

"I'll help you, Melody," Carrie offered. She jumped up from the couch where she had been reading a book and ran to the small table that was kept in one corner of the living room. Together she and Melody carried it outside and set it up beneath the maples. They reset it, and I filled their glasses, and peace was restored.

The casserole was delicious. We had a large glass bowl full of horseradish coleslaw to go with our German pizza. Amanda had brought it. "This coleslaw was catered from the well-known Montgomery's restaurant in Cincinnati," she said. "Our neighbors had a gathering over the weekend, and they gave us this leftover coleslaw." She laughed. "I think they didn't like it either."

It was certainly different. I made sure I ate my small helping with large bites of potatoes and meat. It helped mask the strong flavor.

"It would be good, if we just liked horseradish," Mom remarked. Lowell sniffed at the bowl as he passed it on down the table. "Better eat some," I suggested. "It may be your only chance to eat horseradish coleslaw from Montgomery's."

Lowell shook his head. "I think I'll pass."

"I ate mine while I was still hungry," Ida Mae said. "It wasn't really that bad."

"Poor Christopher got a big helping and he's already wishing he hadn't," Amanda teased. "I heard him gag when he took his first bite."

Christopher laughed. "You most certainly did not."

"That was me," Emily said. "I didn't exactly gag, but I did make a funny sound."

"And all the time I really did think it was Christopher, choking over his coleslaw," Amanda said.

We were all tasting it and voicing our opinions, so after he had eaten his casserole, Wesley decided he would be brave and sample some too. With the first bite his face changed expressions fast. If Christopher hadn't choked, Wesley certainly did.

"Spit it out," someone advised.

"Drink some water, quick!" "Don't throw up, please!" Wesley gulped some water, pushed away his plate, and looked pale. The rest of the children decided not to try it.

"The chickens would probably eat it," I remarked, thinking it was too bad no one was enjoying that big bowlful of coleslaw.

"But they might lay horseradish-flavored eggs," someone called from down the length of the table.

• • •

It was late June, and the daylilies were coming into bloom. We washed the dishes fast, eager to head outside and discover which varieties were blooming for Mom today.

"I have space in one flower bed for three more," I said, drying the dishes while Regina washed. "I want to see what I can find today that I would like to plant there."

"I don't think I'll get any new ones this year," Regina said. "I'm digging out and discarding some of mine that aren't as nice. I'm going to downsize to seventy-five different ones."

"That's funny," I remarked. "When I get three more I'll have seventy-five."

Mom was on her way to the fridge with some leftovers, and she paused to give me a strange look. "I thought you didn't have many daylilies."

"I thought you didn't even want very many," Regina added.

"That was years ago," I explained patiently. "Back then I thought I didn't want flowers that bloom for only one day. I'm wiser now, and I've learned to like them. Besides," I added with a sigh, "with just a few here and a few more there, they've really added up in my flower beds in the last five or ten years."

Dishes done, we gathered up the babies, the smallest children ran along beside us, and we started our daylily stroll. We took a rambling circle through the flower beds near the house, then down the lane, finally ending up in the garden beside the greenhouses. Quite a few varieties were already in full bloom.

There were always old favorites to greet and admire when they bloomed again come June. Their names sounded like music and ripples of laughter and good memories of days long gone: Eloquent Silence, Heart of It All, Comanche Drums, Indian Rhapsody, Violet Becomes You, Ruffled Apricot, Stolen Treasure, Only the Lonely, Last Flight Out, Raspberry Sunshine, and a hundred or two more.

"My Country Melody is blooming, Grandma," Melody called back to Mom as we ambled along the rows in the garden. "It has one flower open today. I saw it this morning."

"Mine is blooming again too," Mom replied. A year or two ago she had given Melody a start of the daylily that shared her name.

"I'm looking for a few tall ones in shades of orange," Amanda remarked as we walked between the rows in the garden. "I'm using those kinds to fill up an area behind the hitching rail."

"I've got some nice peach and orange ones I could share," I offered. "A tall, bright orange one with coppery edges called All Fired Up. Or I could give you a start of Jim's Pick, a pale orange."

"I think All Fired Up would be a good choice for the area where I want to plant these," Amanda decided.

I paused to admire a pinkish daylily. "This one is nice. I believe I'll ask Mom for a start from this plant. Then I'll just need two more."

Amanda turned to look. "Oh, I have that one too. It's called New Series. I can trade you one for a start from your All Fired Up."

"Yes, let's do that," I agreed. I liked the name almost as well as the color. Few things are as much fun as finding a new series of books by an old, beloved author, or discovering a new author and more new series. A pink daylily called New Series needed a place in my garden somewhere, even if something else had to go.

"I have space for only one or two more daylilies," Emily said, "so I want them to be pretty special. Big, ruffled, two-colored. Like Bullfrog Kisses or Jennifer Trimmer or Violet Becomes You."

"All of those are slow growers," Mom said, glancing along the rows. "The plants are still too small to start digging any roots this year."

"I know," Emily replied. "I really should start pouring Miracle-Gro on them each week. Then maybe by next year I could have a start."

The children were running back and forth along the rows, begging for flowers. "You may each pick one daylily that you like," Mom told them, and this satisfied them. They gravely selected their favorites, twisted off the flowers, sometimes breaking buds in the process, and carried their chosen blooms along. This lasted only until we came to the end of the rows, where broken petals and smashed flowers were discarded, and they ran off to play again.

We stopped on the lawn and I pointed at a daylily that had huge pink-and-white flowers with elongated petals. "I remember that one from last year. What's it called?"

"That one is Webster's Pink Wonder," Mom answered. "It's a spider daylily. I happen to like the spider types too."

"I have a few other spiders," I said. Spiders are daylilies that bloom with petals exceptionally long and narrow. The flowers are bigger too. "I find them sort of pretty, in their own spidery way. I want a Webster's Pink Wonder this year too."

Regina eyed the few spider varieties blooming with the others. "It's dreadful to admit it, but I think I want one of those spider varieties sometime. They're growing on me too."

"Is that so dreadful?" I laughed.

"It is. I wasn't planning on planting any spiders. I'm not supposed to like them."

I pulled some tall weeds along the edge of the garden, or tried to. The tops came off in my hands, leaving the roots behind to grow again. It reminded me of something I had once read. An easy way to tell the difference between a weed and an expensive plant, someone wrote, tongue in cheek, is to pull it out. If it comes easily it was your expensive plant.

I tossed the weeds onto a nearby pile. It was getting dry, and pulling weeds was difficult to do in the hard soil, although lack of water didn't deter any of the weeds growing nearby. They all looked healthy and satisfied.

Luella was standing on a gently sloping rock beside the daylilies, and as we watched her she lost her balance. In slow motion she toppled full length across the Strawberry Candy, mowing down buds and blooms as she went.

Ida Mae rushed to pull her out. "Oh, Luella! Right into the middle of the flowers."

Luella wasn't hurt, but she stared at the crushed stems and leaves and looked as if she would cry.

"Never mind, Luella," Mom soothed her. "Most of those flower stems will stand up again. We won't miss the ones that don't."

As we headed back uphill to the house, the schoolboys were on their way down the lane, waving plastic bags. "We're going to the fields to hunt for arrowheads," they called back to us.

KellyAnn and Matthan took off after them, running as fast as they could. Searching for arrowheads sounded more exciting than scrutinizing the different shades and ruffles and extreme pie crusting on the daylilies, as their moms were doing.

The greenhouse was still holding the last of the season's plants, the final fading pots and planters that would soon be hauled off to the auction and sold or allowed to dry up in the heat and discarded. I looked inside when we passed, but didn't stop. The spring magic and excitement was over, but all the work still lingered. I had so many plants at home to care for that it was time I ignored all those free plants begging for a place to grow. If I gave in and took them along I would have to care for them, and summer's heat and the bulk of harvest was just ahead.

• • •

After we finished selecting daylilies, we hauled the wheelbarrow and a shovel to a sloping bank beside the barn. Weeds had taken over this flower bed, and Mom wanted the rocks removed and this particular bank returned to grass that could be mowed.

Using the shovel, and heaving and grunting, I flipped the heavy rocks over and into the wheelbarrow, and Mom and Emily hauled them to an area near the porch, beneath the maples. That was where we would build a fire and roast hot dogs and have a picnic each summer before the children went back to school. With these large rocks we planned to fashion a rustic fire ring.

Amanda and Regina heaved the rocks into a circle around the charred area, and as the circle grew, Corey and Janessa leaped from rock to rock in a happy merry-go-round of motion. Alisha seated David on one of the rocks, and he kicked his feet against the ground as if he would like to jump up and run after them, if only he could.

I carried some of the last, smaller rocks across the lawn and gave them to Amanda, who was slipping the final ones into position. A twist here and a tuck there, and the rocks lay firm and solid on the earth.

At last we all stood back to admire our newly fashioned fire ring. "Now it's ready to build a fire and roast hot dogs," we said.

Matthan, who had by now returned from hunting arrowheads and was the contented owner of a handful of smooth and shiny stones he called arrowheads, was as happy about the fire ring as we were. But when I told him it was almost time to go home, he was indignant.

"Home? It's not time to go home yet."

"Yes, it is. I'm going to start getting our things together."

"But, Mom, aren't we going to roast hot dogs yet before we go?"

"No, not today," I replied.

Matthan found this hard to believe. Of what use was a brand-new fire ring if we weren't going to let him roast a hot dog immediately, if not sooner? "Will we roast some next week?" he persisted.

"I don't know, Matthan. Probably not. But we will sometime yet before school starts."

And with that promise he had to be satisfied.

BETWEEN TUESDAYS

Two days later, baby Steven was born to Joel and Ida Mae. Bradley was happy to have a brother, and Melody and Luella were happy to have a new baby at their house. He weighed eight pounds, measured twenty-one inches long, and had a head covered with lots of coal-black hair.

"Two little boys born in June," Mom marveled. "Before Conrad and Steven arrived there were no June birthdays in our family."

There were twelve boys now, with Cody the oldest of the grandchildren and Steven the youngest. There were ten girls too. We never, ever wondered why summer Tuesdays at Mom's resembled a chaotic sort of circus.

• • •

"Christ liveth in me: and the life which I now live in the flesh I live by the faith of the Son of God, who loved me, and gave himself for me."

GALATIANS 2:20

JULY

Pandemonium: The Tuesday Moments

JULY BROUGHT HEAT and high summer and the beginning of harvest. It brought peaches and pickles, blueberries and raspberries, beans and tomatoes, all ready to pick and can. I headed to the packing shed to look for zucchini. "To make zucchini relish," I told my sisters. "Four batches of it." They raised their eyebrows.

In the shed I filled a plastic bag until it bulged with zucchini and lugged it to the carriage. A sure sign that the seasons had shifted to summer was when my carriage was filled with produce instead of plants.

Peppers were growing in the field directly below the shed, and I went there next, searching for some seconds to fill another bag. The plants hung heavy with peppers, and the rows were long and curved along the gradual slope of the field. Here and there I found a pepper with a spot or blemish, or one too misshapen to pack and ship.

I filled my bag and my apron too. Hot and tired, I toiled back up to the shed just as Christopher came by for another stack of buckets. "I was taking only the seconds," I said, in case he asked.

"There's a box partly filled with seconds somewhere here in the shed," he said. "You can have those too."

After another search I located the box. I could have saved myself so much work if I'd found it first. I sighed and hauled it along to the house. Some of my sisters were sure to want a few peppers too.

I heard voices in the grape tomato greenhouse and peered in. Long green vines grew nearly to the roof, held up by stakes and twine, and little crimson tomatoes dangled among the leaves. The pungent odor of the plants drifted out on the hot greenhouse air, along with the schoolboys' chatter. They were somewhere at the other end, dragging buckets along the rows, filling their hands with the firm little tomatoes, and dreaming of what they would do with the dollars they earned.

Mom had put up her hammock over the weekend, and it swung between two maples near the trampoline. Carrie was curled up there with a pillow and a book. Corey and Makayla were near the swings, pulling up clumps of grass as I passed. "What are you doing?" I asked, for they were piling it under the slide and patting it gently into circles.

"We're making bird nests," Makayla explained, eyes sparkling.

"Big bird nests," Corey added with a grin.

In the house I began peeling peaches for dinner from a boxful Regina had brought. Regina was making a taco quiche, Emily was mixing sauce for cheese potatoes, and Mom was arranging chicken nuggets on a cookie sheet. I felt fortunate to be peeling peaches, because as usual we were talking so much it was hard to remember what we were doing.

It wasn't that our topics were of any momentous importance, it was simply a sharing of daily moments, thoughts, lessons learned or in the process of being learned. As long as we breathe there are things to learn, and sometimes we can benefit from sisters' lessons too. We talked about our children, our day-to-day lives, what we were reading or thinking or experiencing, and all the other ordinary things five sisters talk about when they are together. If "home is where our story begins," home is certainly also where many of our stories are told. And retold and thrice told.

After a while Regina began wandering around the kitchen mumbling to herself.

"What are you doing?" we asked, staring.

"I can't find my cookbook," she explained, looking under bags and poking into corners and searching every surface. "Where could I have put it?"

"It's definitely a Tuesday moment," I said with a laugh. "Tuesday moments" came into being the other year, the day Amanda was trying to cut a dress for KellyAnn amid much noise and chatter. Her tape measure was missing the first two inches and she was holding it up and peering at it. "If my tape measure is missing two inches at the top, should I add two inches to the bottom before I cut the fabric?" she asked Emily.

Emily blinked at the tape measure Amanda was dangling before her eyes. "I would sure hope so," she replied.

We all laughed. "It's a Tuesday moment," we said, and that's how we've explained them ever since, those moments of blankness when even the most obvious eludes one's memory in the commotion.

"Oh, here it is." Regina pulled her cookbook from behind a pile of other things. "Now what do I do next?"

The door opened, and Carrie ran in, tears spilling down her cheeks. She looked terrified and was choking back sobs. "Carrie, what happened to upset you so?"

Carrie leaned against Regina and wept. The door crashed behind a pile of boys, in the midst of which was Lowell, holding a huge, ugly crayfish with two-inch antennae and lobster-like claws. The boys were excited and laughing.

Carrie wasn't. "Lowell held that thing in front of my eyes."

For Carrie had been peacefully reading in the hammock when the boys came up from the fishing hole with this trophy that had somehow appeared on Tristan's line. Lowell had swooped to the hammock and flaunted the creature between Carrie's eyes and her book. The book flew, the tears came, and Carrie fled to the house.

As moms, we weren't sure whether or not it was funny. Carrie's fright was understandable, for none of us wanted to get too close to the ugly thing. But the boys thought they had a prize. They clustered around it, watching the beast scrabbling around the bottom of the container.

At last we ushered them and their new pet out the door. "And don't use it to scare any more girls," we ordered.

The dinner table was stretched long and filled the room. The children ate as all hungry children do—a lot. The men came in warm and ready to sit down and rest their feet. They drank lots of water with ice cubes melting in the tumblers and causing condensation to bead on the sides. We women all sat down too, glad another meal was on the table.

"Say, Christopher," said Duane as they were eating, "how much are we paying these boys to pick grape tomatoes this year?"

"About fifty cents a bucket sounds like a good deal, don't you think?" Christopher replied.

A storm of protest erupted. Cries of "Poor pay!" and "I quit!" and "That's not nearly enough" ran along the row of boys.

Duane and Christopher grinned. "You mean you're expecting more than fifty cents a five-gallon bucket?" they asked, pretending to be surprised.

Later that afternoon, the schoolboys trudged up the hill again, hot, flushed, but happy. They were waving dollar bills, or patting shirt pockets that crinkled satisfactorily. "Did you get more than fifty cents a bucket after all?" Emily asked her boys.

"Yes, Mom, we certainly did," Tristan and Travis assured her.

"I knew we'd get more than that," Bradley said. "They were just teasing us."

"Well, Tristan and Travis were looking sort of worried at the table," Emily explained. "I could tell they weren't sure whether or not Christopher was serious."

In the usual pandemonium of gathering up all our children and sorting out all our stuff and trying to remember not to forget anything, Emily said to Mom, "When are you going to be old enough that you'll tell us to just stay at home?"

"Or at least to come one at a time," Amanda added.

"I'm not there yet," Mom said, laughing. "I'm not there yet."

I hauled my basket to the carriage just as Emily and Amanda were leaving. Their horse started off patiently, and the wagon was full of assorted bags, boxes, and happy children waving goodbye. Wesley and Travis took off their straw hats and waved them at Matthan as they all yelled, "Goodbye! Goodbye!"

• • •

Charlotte trotted peacefully through the early morning cool-
ness, taking us to Ida Mae's house for our Tuesday with her. By
next week newborn Steven would be old enough for his first
excursion to Mom's house, but today we would go to him.

Charlotte was peaceful this time, but inside the carriage it
was not. Matthan had insisted on bringing his toy bow and ar-
rows, and they appeared periodically in my line of vision, being
long and awkward.

"Please put those things in the back," I said at last. "I don't
like them in front of my eyes when I'm driving. I'm afraid I'll
wreck."

Matthan retired rather sulkily to the back seat, and Alisha
shrieked. "Stop, Mom, stop! I dropped my pack of gum on
the road."

I stopped Charlotte and Alisha ran back to get it. "Put it
in the back too," I sighed. "We're having a hard time getting
anywhere."

"Do we have the fly swatter?" Matthan demanded, poking
his head over the seat.

"It's in the basket," I said. "But you're not supposed to hit
their puppy with it. Just wave it around."

"I know that." Matthan found Twig, the big, black puppy at
Ida Mae's home, way too big and scary, and a fly swatter was
language Twig understood. "Did I tell Melody about my parakeets already?"

Matthan's parakeets were an answer to a little boy's prayer.
He had first asked for some about a month ago, begging for
pretty little birds to keep in the house in a cage. "Maybe when
you're a little older," I replied, actually meaning, "I hope you'll
forget about it between now and then."

But a woman we knew dropped in one day, looking for a home for her four parakeets. I watched Matthan's face as she talked. He could understand English as well as anyone, and his eyes had begun to sparkle until his whole face glowed. Who was I to stand in the way of a little boy's dream, or to deny that it was an answer to a little boy's prayer?

So Matthan now had four of the prettiest little parakeets, and he wanted to tell Melody about them. "If you already told her I suppose you can tell her again," I said.

When I carried my things up the walk to Ida Mae's house, Twig came to greet me. He was a large black bundle of puppy pranks, and it was easy to see that a kitten would not have fared well on the same property, even if Twig only meant to play.

He followed me to the door and nosed his way just inside the kitchen. "Stay there," I said, and he obeyed. He flopped down with his head and front paws across the threshold and his body holding the door ajar.

"That's as far as he's allowed inside," Ida Mae explained. "It seems to make him feel that he's in here with us, without actually having him indoors."

I lifted an ice cream bucket of macaroni salad from my basket. "Is there room in your fridge for this? It should be kept cold."

"It's full up here," Ida Mae said, "but you may take it to the basement."

I shoved things around in the fridge downstairs to make room for it. The younger children were swooping circles on the concrete floor with trikes and assorted riding toys. "I'll have to bring Matthan down here to play," I remarked. "Then he won't have to worry about the puppy."

Luella gave me a big smile as she sailed past, followed by Janessa. "Twig may not come down here."

Baby Steven slept most of the day, sometimes in his soft little bed, but more often in someone's arms. He tolerated all our racket very well and woke only when he wanted to eat. The little girls kept the little rocker occupied as they demanded turns to hold him.

When Laura Ingalls Wilder wrote, "It is the sweet, simple things of life which are the real ones after all,"[1] she must have meant babies to cuddle, sisters to talk with, little children running back and forth, and boys playing with baseballs and gloves and laughing. She must have meant homes with a bit of earth surrounding them, with blue skies above and green grass to mow and gardens to plant and harvest. She must have meant all that and so much more. Because so far as I can tell, faith in the creator God of the universe and the sweet, simple things are what bring genuine happiness and serenity of spirit after all.

We wanted to see the rooms upstairs that Ida Mae had been painting earlier that year, so when she offered us a tour we all traipsed upstairs. We oohed and aahed at the freshly painted rooms, and stuck our sisterly noses into every corner, admiring deep closets, spacious areas, and the clean, fresh paint job.

"So this is Bradley's brown room," Mom observed. "I wasn't sure how it would look, but I like it."

"I used paint a shade lighter than he wanted, but he likes it," Ida Mae said. "Then I painted the walls brown only part of the way up, and sponge-painted brown on white the rest of the way."

"It's nice that way," I said. "I like it too."

There was more sponge painting done in the bathroom and in the girls' room. "Oh, pale pink," Emily said. "Melody, I like your room."

"And here you would have just the right place for a window seat," Regina declared, as we paused in the lavender master bedroom. She pointed. "Beneath those two windows."

"I thought about it," Ida Mae admitted. "But I wasn't sure if it would work so I didn't mention it."

"It should work fine if you would build a base between those walls," Regina said.

"A base with drawers in it," I added. "I'm still waiting for a window seat like that in one of my upstairs rooms."

"In one of the gables of our upstairs there's a perfect place for a window seat," Regina said. "I'm still dreaming too."

On the landing where the stairs came up, a recliner was placed in front of a single window. "And here I want floor-to-ceiling bookshelves someday," Ida Mae said with a smile.

"The painting may be finished, but I can see there's still a lot of work before you're done," Mom said as we started downstairs.

The children were no longer playing in the basement or following us around upstairs. They came indoors now, and most of them were wearing bright splotches of orange in their hair. "We picked marigolds in my garden," Melody said. "I helped everyone put some in their hair."

We talked in desultory fashion, jumping from one subject to the next, and landed upon the subject of artists, for Mom was sorting through some of Ida Mae's cards as she talked. "Here's a card with one of Marjolein Bastin's paintings on the front," she pointed out. "She's my favorite artist."

"Do you like her paintings even better than Thomas Kinkade's?" I asked, Thomas Kinkade being not only my favorite artist, but the only one I recognized, since I am no connoisseur of art.

The mention of Thomas Kinkade brought about, in our conversational wanderings, mention of the sign of the fish, with which he had earmarked each painting, and on to the origin of that particular sign as a Christian symbol.

"I just happened to notice the sign of the fish on a vehicle recently," Mom commented. "I wonder how long ago it became symbolic of Christianity?"

Didn't it start with the earliest disciples after Jesus was crucified? We tossed that question around and thought it probably had, for during times of persecution they used it in order to learn who was a Christian. When meeting someone whose loyalties they weren't sure of, they would draw a curved line in the sand or soil with one foot while they talked. If the other person was a disciple too, that person would understand immediately and draw another curved line, completing the picture of a fish. In that way they could tell who was also a disciple of Christ.

"And to someone who didn't believe, and wasn't aware of the meaning, the line in the sand didn't mean anything," Regina concluded.

"Except as a few aimless scribbles," Emily added.

We thought it over in silence for a while, each pondering what being a Christian during times of persecution would mean and what it would require of us. Being a Christian, which really means being a disciple of Jesus Christ, is so much a part of our lives that to us there seems to be no other way to live.

But then we have to be careful not to fall into the ditch on other side, the one where we take everything for granted—including our freedom—and live without making worship, gratitude, discipleship, and obedience to Christ an integral part of who we are and why we live as we do.

It was a matter, I decided, of renewing one's commitment with a series of daily choices, daily decisions. To voluntarily choose to be like Christ, whatever happens; to get up and try again after failing. A New Testament passage comes to mind: "Therefore, brethren, stand fast, and hold the traditions which ye have been taught, whether by word, or our epistle. Now our Lord Jesus Christ himself, and God, even our Father, which hath loved us, and hath given us everlasting consolation and good hope through grace, Comfort your hearts, and stablish you in every good word and work" (2 Thessalonians 2:15-17).

It is a comfort that as we stand fast, as we cling to the traditions of being Christlike and obedient to that which he taught, and faithful where he has placed us, he would give us everlasting consolation, good hope through his grace, and comfort for our hearts.

• • •

Soon it was dinnertime. It was the schoolboys' turn to eat outside, and they greeted this announcement with shouts of assent.

"We can take our plates back to the deck," Bradley told his cousins. "It will be fun to eat there."

"Close the gate to the steps," Ida Mae called after them. "Or Twig will get into your food."

We served some croutons to go with the chicken, but Corey was not impressed. He sniffed at the crisp cubes and made a face. "Ugh. Dog food. I don't eat dog food."

Amanda had brought several bags of Heat Wave chips. "The girls won't eat them. Does someone like hot foods?"

The boys thought they were up to the challenge and sampled them. The chips were good, they decided, and they ate as many as they could. In between mouthfuls of chips they kept the water pitcher empty. "Whew! Fill my glass again. I need more water to wash down these chips. Whew!"

"This macaroni salad is good," Amanda commented as we ate.

Farther up the table I heard her words, and was amazed. Something I'd made had turned out good? Was there still hope for some improvement after all these years of more or less trial-and-error cooking?

Later, we finished the dishes, shortened the table, tidied the sink and kitchen, and made sure the boys had left nothing on the deck. "Now," Regina said, "I want to see Ida Mae's hostas yet before it's time to go home."

I hung up the dishcloth. "I'll go with you."

Mom came up from the basement with a box she'd stowed in the fridge that morning. "And I will have to prepare this fruit after we come back inside. I brought all the fixings for the children to have fruit cones before we go home."

There were plastic containers of raspberries, blueberries, and strawberries in the box, and bags of grapes, nectarines, and kiwis. "I could start getting it ready, Grandma," Alisha offered.

"That would be nice," Mom decided. "You can wash the grapes and berries and halve the grapes."

"I'll help you, Alisha," Carrie decided. "It'll be fun. I can cut the grapes in half."

We left them both absorbed in their domestic duties and went outside. Ida Mae carried Steven along, using a light blanket to shield his face from the bright sunshine.

The schoolboys were at play in the woods when we came to the back of the house, and Twig was bounding along with them. "He must think today is the happiest day of his life," Ida Mae remarked.

Behind the house the ground stayed moist, and the shade from the nearby woods kept the area cool. Here a profusion of hostas flourished. Some were huge, with leaves striped, variegated, and dappled. Some were medium-sized, and some were tiny, with rounded leaves splashed with color. It was worth a walk to admire them.

When we got back to the house Alisha and Carrie were busy chopping. We sat at the table and helped, filling a bowl with sliced strawberries, kiwis, halved grapes, and diced nectarines.

"I saw this in a magazine and have been wanting to try it," Mom explained, bringing out boxes of waffle cones and cans of Reddi-Wip. "Today seemed like a good time to see how we like it. Then I'll have an idea how it would work to take along to Noah and Christine's campout later this summer."

It was only an hour or two since we had dried and put away the last of the dinner dishes, but you wouldn't have guessed it to see the children lining up beside Mom to have their cones filled. She scooped the fruit mixture into their waiting cones with a big spoon, then they moved on to Emily and Alisha, who held the Reddi-Wip cans upside down and spiraled graceful whorls of cream on top.

The little girls were first, and they clutched the cones in their hands as they headed for the door. "You can eat on the porch," Ida Mae agreed, holding open the door for Melody and Janessa.

We were piling fruit into the boys' cones when several shrieks sounded on the porch. They were of the kind that turn moms' knees to jelly and make them imagine many terrible things in the few seconds it takes to investigate.

Melody and Janessa ran inside, crying. "Twig ate our cones," Melody wailed.

"He ate my cone," Janessa agreed, between sniffles.

"We'll make others for you," Mom consoled them. "There's still fruit in the bowl."

"And here are more cones," Emily added.

"That puppy is not my favorite thing these days," Ida Mae sighed.

The empty bowl was left behind when the children were all outside again. The cone boxes and wrappers were strewn about, and the kitchen looked as if a small cyclone had hit it. With resignation we set about putting it right.

We had just finished when more sounds of distress reached our ears. Alisha came limping inside, dusty and wiping tears, surrounded by a circle of alarmed children. Melody and Luella were crying hardest.

"Whatever happened now?" I exclaimed as Alisha dragged across the room and sank down on the couch, holding her foot. "Is it broken?"

"It was my swing that broke," Melody sobbed. "I hope Alisha broke her leg for breaking my swing."

Matthan decided to take matters into his own hands and came to the aid of his sister. He pinched Melody for that, and there were more tears, his included.

It took a while until we restored order, comforted and chastened children, and decided Alisha's foot was not broken.

Then we swept the rooms for the last time and gathered our scattered belongings. The children were given their hats and bonnets and told to hop on board. It was time to go home.

"Bye, Grandma," called KellyAnn and Wesley from the wagon as Mom came out on the porch.

"Bye, Grandma," echoed Travis and Makayla and Janessa.

"Goodbye, children," Mom called back. "Next week you come to my house again."

"Yes," agreed Amanda, carrying Ashley to the wagon, "next week we want to go to Grandma's house again."

• • •

It was the last Tuesday in July. David was learning to walk, and he wobbled from Mom to the chair and back again.

It was also little Steven's first day at Mom's house. Oblivious to the noise and racket, he ate and slept and ate again.

Emily had a book about Martha's Vineyard for Mom. "Because I know you've dreamed of going there someday," she said.

A suncatcher inside one window was reflecting rainbowed patches of light. The little colored bows danced on the walls and floor, and on Janessa and Ashley, as Mom fetched the atlas from the desk. "If I ever visit Martha's Vineyard I would go to Nantucket as well," she said. "I wonder how far apart both places are."

"Let's plan a sisters' trip," Emily suggested. "We could travel up the New England coast and visit all those places."

"And take Jerelyn and Alisha along to babysit," Amanda added. Jerelyn and Alisha weren't sure whether they agreed to this. It would be a big job, they thought, protesting.

Mom located Martha's Vineyard on the atlas. "It's not that far away," I said. "We really should visit someday."

"But who's going to finance it?" someone asked, and we came thumping back to planet earth. Babysitters or no babysitters, a sisters' excursion such as we were discussing wasn't anywhere close in our futures.

"At least dreams are free," I said before we turned to more down-to-earth duties, such as choosing food to take to Noah's campout from the menu Christine had made.

"I could buy supplies for s'mores," Emily decided, writing her name on that line.

"Garden tea," I read off the paper. "I'd better let someone else make that. I can't make garden tea that tastes like it should."

"Neither can I," Amanda said, making me think perhaps I wasn't so strange after all.

"I'll do the tea," Regina offered. "I have lots of peppermint, and I don't mind making some for the campout."

I scanned the list of food. "Fresh fruit. I could bring that." Even I should be capable of buying fruit and getting it to the campout while it was still edible.

The children were playing in one of the empty greenhouses and having a wonderful time. "They were making a bit of a mess when I checked on them," Ida Mae said. "But they were playing so nicely I didn't have the heart to make them stop."

They all came up to the house soon after that, and a few of them were carrying plastic pots. Matthan came inside with a droopy succulent. "Mom, could you take care of my flower for me?"

I took the pot with a sigh. The last thing I wanted was another plant of any sort to care for.

While we worked at dinner I told my sisters about the coun-terfeit twenty-dollar bill that had been discovered with the other money at the produce auction where Cody worked three afternoons a week. Someone at the bank had found the bill and returned it to the auction manager.

"Now the boys at the auction have the bill," I said, "and they have decided to see how often they can use it to trick the girls who work at JR's Store." The store was just down the road from the auction and was where the boys bought snacks and other food.

"It might not be so easy," Emily said. She had worked there years ago. "We had to learn how to tell those bills from the real ones."

"But if it's only a twenty it may be easier," Regina said.

"Yes, that's true. We mostly checked the larger bills."

"They've already used it once," I said. "Cody and one of his friends took it to JR's yesterday and bought a pack of jerky. The girl at the cash register took the twenty and started counting out their change. That's when they started laughing and told her she might want to give that twenty a closer look."

"Sort of embarrassing for her," Ida Mae observed.

"Yes, it would be," I agreed. "But now they have the bill back and will try again tomorrow."

Mom shook her head. "They may be able to use it twice, but I doubt they'll get away with it the third time."

Matthan was playing and would never miss his succulent, I was sure. I sneaked it to the greenhouse and put it on the table with the last forlorn-looking specimens. Then I hurried back to the house, pleased to have taken care of that so neatly.

Corey and Melody came running in. "Grandma," Corey began, "do you want us to bring some cantaloupes for dinner?"

Mom thought a little. "Yes, you may bring some to the house. We'll have them with our dessert."

Emily came indoors carrying several peppers and zucchini. "I don't know if those children are going to need any dinner at all. When I was down at the packing shed looking for produce they were all sitting on the wagon, cutting up cantaloupes and eating as many slices as they could."

In the late afternoon Mom brought out a box filled with graham crackers and chocolate bars and marshmallows. "I thought we could try out the fire ring," she said. "Since the children have been asking when they can have a picnic, we'll roast some marshmallows today."

The children ran to drag chairs outside under the trees, and they formed a circle around Mom as she held a match to the paper. "Not so close," she cautioned them. "It will be hot. Move your chairs further back."

We sent the boys to find sticks to use, and by the time they came puffing back waving a handful, the fire was crackling nicely. We had all the supplies for s'mores arranged on a small table. The marshmallows were supersized, and a single one was big enough to use on a whole cracker. I helped Matthan skewer a smaller one onto a stick for his s'more.

KellyAnn pulled one of the big marshmallows from the bag and held it up. "These are big round haybales," she laughed.

Janessa came running. "I want a big haybale too," she cried.

I took one from the bag and gave it to her. She held it like a ball and it filled both of her hands.

Ida Mae finished toasting Luella's marshmallow. It was light brown and bubbly and just right, but Luella didn't think so. "Not like that," she wailed. "It looks gross."

"Did you want it black instead?" Ida Mae asked, perplexed.

I fixed Matthan's s'more for him, with the Hershey's bar sandwiched thick, dark, and gooey between cracker and marshmallow, and smiled to see that instead of toasting her marshmallow, Makayla held it in one hand and ate it like an apple.

I pulled a chair up to the fire ring and sat down. "I'm not that fond of marshmallows. I don't know if I want a s'more."

"Unlike Melody," Ida Mae remarked. "She's on her third marshmallow already. But this one isn't going down very fast."

I was glad I hadn't made a s'more when Matthan came running over with his. "Here, Mom, you may have the rest of mine."

I accepted the sticky and fingerprinted cracker sandwich and eyed it doubtfully. "I suppose I could finish this for you. It doesn't look like you've eaten much of it yet."

I took one bite, then a few more. It didn't taste anything like s'mores were supposed to, so I pulled the crackers apart. "Now I see what's wrong with this thing," I exclaimed.

My sisters looked at me with puzzled faces. "Matthan ate the chocolate and gave me what's left," I explained with a sigh. "And the Hershey's bar is the only reason I'd eat a s'more."

• • •

When the children were all playing again we pulled our chairs around the diminishing fire and sat there, waving aside the last tendrils of smoke and talking idly about not much in particular. Steven drowsed all the while. It was his first experience with a campfire, and he preferred to sleep it away.

We nibbled the last of our s'mores to the clamor of auctioneers in practice. Matthan, Wesley, Corey, KellyAnn, and Melody were all in the hammock not far away, taking turns being an auctioneer. Sometimes they weren't taking turns.

"I've tried to tell the boys that auctioneers don't actually yell so loudly," Emily said. "That they just talk normally and let the loudspeaker do the rest. But they like to be as loud as they can."

"Why do all little boys like auctioneering?" I asked, but it was a question for which no one had an answer. I thought of the days when Matthan would auctioneer all day long, and when he knelt to say his prayers at night he would begin auctioneering instead.

At last we got up to clear away the remains of our afternoon snack, and a sticky mess it was. Marshmallow was smeared on the front door knob, on the table, on children's hands and faces.

Amanda picked up a half-eaten marshmallow that was lying on the ground and gave it to Sheba the dog, who was sniffing around. Sheba took it gingerly between her teeth and carried it a safe distance away. Then she lay down and licked it half-heartedly.

"She's not sure she should eat that much sugar," Amanda laughed.

I looked over at Sheba, who had now taken a tiny bite. I laughed too. "She's thinking that it's hard on her diet, but she'll eat it anyhow."

It was time to go home; all our things were stowed away in my basket. And Matthan came running. "Mom? Mom, where's my flower?"

And hadn't I just a few hours before congratulated myself on my successful solution to the case of the unwanted plant by smuggling it back to the greenhouse?

• • •

*"Thy faithfulness is unto all generations: thou hast estab-
lished the earth and it abideth."*

PSALM 119:90

AUGUST

When Daughter Takes Over Driving Charlotte

SUMMER HAD MATURED into August. It was beautiful that year, with cool, sunny days strung like beads upon a string and ticked off one by one.

This month Alisha decided it was time she had a turn driving Charlotte on the way to Mom's house. I turned over the reins reluctantly. Charlotte was not inclined to move very fast these summer days, but even so, I wasn't sure about the idea.

I sat beside Alisha, nervously aware of every little jerk and squeak and trot as we headed down the winding Lapperell hill.

"Are you braking?"

"Yes, Mom."

I studied Charlotte and her harness and fidgeted. "But the backing strap is tight. She's having to hold back the weight of the carriage. Are you sure you're using the brake?"

"Of course, Mom. It's almost flat. I can't brake any harder."

I fidgeted some more. "Aren't we going a little fast?"

"It's downhill, Mom! Of course she's running!"

We got to the top of the hill at Mom's house at last and I sagged against the back of the seat. "Aah," I sighed. "Whoo."

Alisha gazed at me. "Was it really that bad?"

"No," I admitted. "It really wasn't. You did very well."

• • •

Amanda had a book for Mom to fix. It was *Powerful Promises for Every Woman* by Elizabeth George, and some of its pages were falling out.

That reminded us of the books we had bought on Saturday when Emily, Amanda, and I were at Goodwill, where the books were priced four for a dollar. We probably spent an hour in the book section of that store, browsing through every shelf. And, as we told Mom, we arrived at the checkout with enough books in our carts to cause the woman in line behind us to raise her eyebrows and ask what our husbands were going to say when we came home with that many books.

Amanda assured her that our husbands knew us pretty well by now. I said, "My husband would actually be more surprised if I came home without any books."

We had kept our eyes open for more Elizabeth George books, having read and shared quite a few of hers over the last few years. But we found only one more, *A Woman after God's Own Heart*.

Almost everything, even books, is better when shared with sisters.

A five-gallon bucket of green beans from Mom's garden was waiting on the porch. It was for Regina, whose bean stalks weren't producing much, and I dragged a large white bag into the kitchen that was bulging with another bucketful of beans.

"I hope you want these too," I said. "I've canned all we need for the year."

"I'm happy to have them," Regina assured me. "I haven't canned more than a few quarts yet."

When we poured bucket and bag upon the table, a mountain of green beans bulked there. We gathered knives and bowls and pulled our chairs around, working fast.

The heaps of cleaned and chopped beans grew high in the bowls. "How long your pieces are," I remarked to Emily, looking from hers to the pile of much shorter pieces I had chopped into my bowl. "I wonder how Regina wants them."

"Let me get my tape measure," Regina said, hiding a smile. "I want them to be exactly one inch long." She stared at the piles of beans we had ready for jars. "These are too long," she said, pointing at Emily's. "And yours are much too short," she said to me.

We pretended to be miffed.

"Those beans are fine," Regina said, laughing with us. "They'll taste the same no matter what size they are. My summer is pretty hectic," she added, "and the size of the beans I'm canning couldn't bother me less. Sometimes I'm not sure what all is happening in a day, or if I'm coming or going. It's this having all six children at home just now."

She paused momentarily from pouring the beans into a bigger bowl and asked, "Or do I have seven?"

This was certainly a Tuesday moment. No, we assured her between gales of laughter, the last time we counted you still had six children.

Ida Mae walked past with Steven nestled on her shoulder, his little black head tucked close to her ear. With one eye open and one eye shut, he blinked owlishly at us and our merriment. "See, you know we're worth it all," he seemed to be saying. "Even if there are days when you wonder if you'll still be sane by the time we're all grown up."

Perhaps we will be. And a day at Mom's house every week, to remind ourselves how blessed we are to have this structure for our lives, will certainly help.

Today Amanda brought her Big Shot machine, as well as the small steel shapes, called dies, used to cut paper, and a pile of colored card stock. Alisha and Jerelyn were soon busy at the table too, but they weren't readying green beans for canning. They were making die cuts out of the colored papers, changing dies and papers, and trying to decide which shapes and colors to use next.

It all sounded like Greek to me. "I see I have no choice anymore about getting involved in stamp art and things," I said a little gloomily. "Not with Alisha wanting to learn everything she can about it."

"Indeed you don't," Amanda laughed. "And I'm going to help Alisha learn all she wants to."

I was only too happy to let her, I reflected, thinking that even cleaning beans was a great deal more fun than making cards.

"After all, it's such a fun hobby to have," Emily agreed.

"A good way to relax," Regina said. She gave me a sharp glance. "Although you'd better make sure to leave your pens and typewriter at home."

"Don't think about trying to teach us how to write in exchange for us teaching Alisha about stamping and card-making," Emily added.

"But you don't know how much fun it is," I objected. "Such a good way to relax too, sitting down at a desk and writing."

"Relaxing!" my sisters yelped, almost in one voice. "That's not possible." They agreed, with a variety of insulting comments, that writing would be sure to have the opposite effect on them and leave them less than mentally sound.

"This is so relaxing," Alisha murmured, cranking the handle of the Big Shot.

Carrie leaned over the table. "But your paper isn't moving through," she pointed out, concerned. "Nothing is happening."

"How relaxing," Alisha exclaimed, tongue in cheek, and she and Carrie giggled as they fixed the problem.

• • •

Ida Mae shared some extra solar glasses, with which to watch the upcoming eclipse. "I got plenty when I ordered," she said.

"I would take two," I said, glad that one of my sisters was so organized. Of course we wanted to watch the eclipse, but so far I had neglected to buy any of the advertised solar glasses.

"I would take several as well," Regina added, as I went to get my wallet to pay for mine.

• • •

The schoolboys came in for dinner with wet, muddy feet and pants, and happy faces. Bradley showed us some small pieces of raw meat cupped in his palm.

"We butchered the bluegills and chubs we caught today," Tristan explained.

"And here's a crawdad," Bradley said, holding up one of the pieces. "These may be good to eat too."

"But did you know how to get them ready to eat?" I asked in surprise.

"Oh yes," Bradley replied. "I learned to clean fish at a camp-out this summer."

The girls were unimpressed with bits of raw meat in dirty, boyish hands. "Just take it outside again," Jerelyn begged.

The boys weren't listening. "Grandma," they called, "Grandma, may we make a fire in the fire ring to cook this meat?"

When Mom gave her permission, the boys' moms persuaded them to wait until after dinner to try out their great culinary skills. The bits of meat were carefully laid away until after our meal, and five boys lined up at the washbowl to scrub remarkably dirty hands.

While they ate they discussed the possibility of naming their little fishing hole, and what it should be called. "Minnow Meat Lake," suggested one of them.

"Crawdad Hole Lake," decided someone else.

Wesley had other problems. "Mom! Mom, my throat hurts," he said.

"I'm the doctor," said Lowell, beside him. "Say, 'Aah.'"

"Aah," obliged Wesley, his mouth full of meat and macaroni. "Ack, Wesley! Empty your mouth first," said Lowell.

• • •

We were nearly finished eating when Emily asked, "Wesley, do you have something in your ear, or what do I see?"

Wesley turned his head, and his trademark grin, part mischief and part innocence, made his dark eyes shine. "I'm going to grow a watermelon plant there," he explained, showing us the watermelon seed he had placed in his ear.

Emily was a little alarmed. "Better take it out before it slips further in."

"I'll help you," Makayla offered. On her knees on the bench, she reached in and nimbly removed the seed from Wesley's ear.

• • •

The silicone cupcake papers appeared again that noon. I showed them to Amanda. "It's your turn to wash the dishes, isn't it?"

"I believe so. Why?"

"I thought of you yesterday when I was wondering what to make," I said. "Then I baked cupcakes in these papers."

Amanda looked thoughtful. "I should use mine again too sometime. About the time it's your turn to wash the dishes."

We laughed. Later, when Amanda's back was turned as she worked at the sink, I tiptoed around the table, gathering up all the dirty papers. From the beginning, I'd had no intention of making Amanda wash them. I took the pile and hid it near the bottom of my basket and went to dry the dishes.

The pile of dishes dwindled fast. "I would rather wash these than dry them anyhow," Amanda remarked, holding up a silicone paper I had missed. "So you're really getting the worst part of the deal."

She turned to stare at the nearly cleared table. "By the way, where are the others?"

I gazed at the table too, and made a usual clever reply. "Uh," I said.

"Now isn't that funny?" Amanda gave me a sidelong glance. She took a circle around the table, then sneaked to the middle room and began rummaging through my basket.

"Some people sure are nosy," I complained to no one in particular.

She emerged, flourishing the stack of cupcake papers in my face. "I really don't mind washing these."

At noon we asked Christopher how the "battle of the bill" was coming along. Or more specifically, who had won the most points—the boys from the auction with their counterfeit bill, or the girls running the cash register at JR's Store.

"Well, I used it Wednesday to buy a hat," Christopher answered. He told us how the girl at the cash register had been counting out his change when he suggested she might want to take a closer look at the twenty he had just handed over. "I think they'll be more suspicious of us now. But one of the other boys is going to try again next week."

"But I really doubt they'll take that twenty a third time," Mom said.

"I sort of doubt it too," Christopher laughed. "They've now started checking every single twenty we give them."

Whoever first used that twenty at the auction probably never dreamed how much fun the boys were going to have with it before it up ended in the dumpster.

• • •

Meanwhile, Bradley, Tristan, and Dean had built a small fire and were coaxing the languid flames to cook their bits of fish. They had a great audience, from their cousins on the trampoline, who gave them much outrageous advice, to the younger ones who crowded around to watch.

Bradley hauled the little children's table close to the fire ring, then he and Travis stabbed the bits of meat onto sharp sticks. They hung over the rocks, waving away smoke and willing the reluctant flames to roast their prized catch.

Luella fetched salt and pepper shakers from the house and set them on the table, just as the boys decided the charred and incredibly unappetizing-looking flakes of meat were ready to eat.

They gulped it down and pronounced it good. We looked the other way.

The verse for Tuesday on Mom's daily Bible verse calendar proclaimed: "Yea, Lord: I believe that thou art the Christ, the Son of God" (John 11:27).

That says it all, I thought. There is nothing more important than to begin one's journey of faith by saying "Thou art Christ, the Son of God."

. . .

The August afternoons were warm and slow-paced. A heat haze often hung over the long, low hills across the fields, and the kitchen was hot from cooking. When dishes were done we headed to the front porch, pleasantly weary and ready to sit down.

Here the trees shaded away much of the heat from the blazing sunshine, and a breeze was almost always frolicking through the branches. Ferns and begonias and coleus were outgrowing the edges of their pots, and the rockers and glider were inviting.

The last brood of wrens was chitchatting in the birdhouse as we sat down, and the children were running and playing under the trees. The heat never seemed to bother them.

"*Die Botschaft* wasn't in the mail yesterday," Mom said, pulling out a chair at the porch table. "I'm used to having it show up on Monday, and I miss it when it doesn't come."

"Should I go check the mail now, Grandma?" Jerelyn asked. "It might have come today."

"Yes, if you don't mind. I'd appreciate that."

I yawned. Emily was yawning too. "I think I need some coffee," she said.

"Yes, but it's too hot for coffee," I replied, turning the page of a magazine I'd brought to the porch.

Emily went back indoors, and before long she returned with a mug that steamed with fragrance. "Oh, that smells good," I said. "I really do need some too."

"I would have brought you some, but I thought you said it's too hot for coffee," Emily said.

"I know. Never mind, I'll just smell yours." Not only was it too hot, I was too lazy to return to the kitchen and make a cup.

One kitten remained from the nest in the barn and seemed likely to stay. On Tuesdays it was a smothered kitten indeed. At the moment Carrie, Melody, and KellyAnn were holding it and misting it with a flea spray while Corey, Wesley, and Matthan watched. They were waiting for their turn to hold the kitten, which purred from all the attention.

Noah and Christine's annual campout had gone off as planned, and we discussed that too. As always, there had been much food, much talk round the campfire, and little sleep. There were sky lanterns and balloons for the children, and—their favorite campout toys—hundreds of glowsticks. They fastened those around arms and legs and necks, in their hair, and on their clothes, and went running around in the darkness. From a distance it created a most astonishing sight, those scores of colored lights bobbing around in the air like giant fireflies gone neon.

Jerelyn returned from the mailbox and parked her bike under the trees. She walked to the porch carrying two pieces of junk mail.

"Oh, Jerelyn," Mom said. "So *Die Botschaft* wasn't in the mail today after all?"

"I brought you this," Jerelyn said, handing Mom the two fliers she carried. Then, with a grin, she walked back to her bike and reached into the box. "Oh, and I have this too," she said, pulling out the heavy newspaper.

Peace serenaded us there, for the moment, along with our chatter and the rustle of pages as we browsed through the familiar newspaper to find out what was happening in other communities.

The girls played in the hammock—until the boys came and chased them out. The girls clambered onto the trampoline, and just as they were bouncing high enough for it to be fun, the boys left the hammock and climbed up on the trampoline. After that the girls jumped down and ran for the hammock again, only to be pursued after a minute by the boys.

This went on until the girls' laughter changed to complaints. They went into a huddle to decide what to do, and then dashed off down the lane to the water hole, leaving the boys in the hammock staring after them.

Before we quite knew what was happening, the boys were also galloping down the lane like a herd of horses. Perhaps they were all going to fish peacefully and splash in the water. Moms can hope.

Soon Melody and Carrie came toiling back up the hill in tears. "The boys won't let us play at the water hole," they wailed.

Emily offered to go with them to investigate. "I shooed the boys off to play in the creek behind the barn," she admitted when she returned to the porch.

"That's all right," Regina assured her. "If they didn't want to play nicely they could go find something else to do."

"They were trying to make some sort of excuses about the girls running away every time they came near," Emily said. "But they looked really sheepish when I asked why they don't play where the girls aren't. That's when they decided the creek would be a nice spot to spend some time."

And the youngest children soon returned to playing peacefully in the shade of the maples.

Die Botschaft proved to be mentally challenging enough for me, but after a while Mom and Ida Mae were stressing over a difficult Sudoku puzzle. "I'm so glad I don't have to do Sudokus," I reminded them.

"It's such a fun challenge, if one can just get the numbers right," Mom said, writing down another. "No, that's not right either." She closed the book. "Luella, do you think it's time for some candy?"

Luella beamed. "Yes, yes. Jelly beans."

"I have some jelly beans for you today," Mom agreed. "Let me get them."

Luella tagged along to the pantry shelves. "Can I pass them out?"

Steven and Ashley took long naps there on the porch each Tuesday afternoon, cradled in willing arms. When they were awake Steven was happy to oblige us by smiling more easily, and Ashley was learning to sit by herself.

Our conversation rambled on to upcoming surgeries, some of which we had read about in *Die Botschaft*, and about the possibility of a lung transplant being successful, and the various procedures for heart operations, and which one would be better.

On the glider behind us, Jerelyn and Alisha exchanged glances. "Surgeries!" Alisha exclaimed, sounding disgusted.

It wasn't the most interesting of conversations, I suppose, but it did remind me of a woman who, as she was dying of a lung disease, would tell people, "I'm dying, but that's okay. I've learned to know Jesus, and he's going to take care of me. So it's okay."

It was a good thought, both for the lazy afternoons and for the busy harvest days. If we learn to know Jesus, we can echo the woman's words: "He's going to take care of me, and it will be okay."

Amanda had found a length of miniature fencing at a yard sale and had brought it along for Regina. "I thought maybe you'd want to use it in your miniature gardens."

Regina examined the fence. It was made of small sticks and twine. "I think I could use it. If you're sure you don't want it."

"I'm not starting any fairy gardens," Amanda replied. "I don't need one more hobby."

"I made a miniature garden in our old grill," Regina said. "I'll enjoy it from now until spring, and then I'll sell it."

"You should make a few this size," I suggested, tapping one of the round, bowl-like pots in the center of the table. "These would sell really well."

"Yes, I know, but the fairy garden furnishings are so expensive," Regina said. "I couldn't make a lot."

"We should start looking at thrift shops," Mom remarked. "Likely we could find a nice variety of different things."

Corey peeped up from between two planters on the edge of the porch, and his eyes held a happy gleam. "Grandma has a fairy garden," he announced to two of his cousins beside him. He pointed to a bowl that held a few dainty plantings and a tiny ceramic bridge and path and table.

Yes, indeed, miniature gardening is the newest hobby, and one that is biting young and old alike. I don't think I should try to resist it anymore. Let's see, what would I need to plant my first fairy garden . . .

"You know what, Regina?" Emily called across the porch. "My boys are turning out to be just like you."

"Like me?" Regina sounded startled. "What do you mean? How are they like me?"

"They came home last week with the leaves of seven varieties of succulents," Emily sighed. "They pinched them off the last pots in the greenhouse. And Tristan was begging to buy one of the pots that are still left."

"Oh," Regina laughed, "they do sound a little like me."

• • •

Later in the month we exchanged stories about watching the solar eclipse that had occurred on August 21st. Mom was especially fascinated by the little moon shadows she had seen.

"We saw them too," I said. "We called them scallops. Or little waves." At the dimmest point of the eclipse, when an afternoon twilight descended, the last of the light through the leaves overhead made the dearest little scalloped shadows over parts of the lane.

"They were all over the grass here, and on the porch under the trees," Mom said. "It was so interesting to see them."

"We didn't see any moon-shaped shadows," Amanda said. "But we did hear some crickets begin to chirp."

In church on Sunday one of the ministers had used the approaching eclipse as an illustration for his text, which was Matthew 25, the parable of the ten young women with their lamps. The minister knew the eclipse was approaching, he said in his sermon, but he was still caught unprepared. He had forgotten it would be the following day, and now he had no solar glasses with which to watch the moon pass before the sun. And while it would be disappointing not to be able to watch the eclipse, he pointed out, how much more disappointing it would be to have failed to prepare for Christ's return and to be found not ready when that day came.

"He had three pairs of solar glasses before the eclipse began," Mom said. "So many people wanted to give him a pair."

We also discussed someone's observation that when Jesus ascended to heaven, everyone stood outside looking up, watching him go. Wouldn't this be a good time for him to return, while we all stood outside, looking up into the sky?

But now the eclipse was over. Obviously, Jesus didn't return, and we will all go on, being faithful in the spot where he has placed us.

• • •

So the Tuesday afternoons of August drowsed away, to the quiet back-and-forth movements of rockers and gliders, the clink of glasses on the wrought iron table, and the voices and laughter of the children at play nearby. Scores of tiny flower flies hovered before skimming away, breezes rustled through countless leaves overhead, and the air was languorous with the scent of late summer and harvest.

We sometimes mentioned briefly the work we might be doing at home. "I really should be cleaning my house," Amanda remarked once. "It needs a thorough scrubbing."

"And I should be washing the windows at home," I agreed. "They are all so dirty."

But dirty houses can always wait. A score of years from now we will never regret the time we took to sit on Mom's porch, where the flowers bloomed and the shade was cool even at midday. Tomatoes and beans and corn were ripening in the gardens, but they could wait until another day. Or another week. Because this was sister-time, and these hours would never come again.

"How lovely to put a bookmark in the frenzy of our lives—to spend . . . hours with . . . dear friends," wrote Gloria Gaither in the book *Friends through Thick and Thin*.[2] These are the days we slow down and spend time just being together. Mom and my sisters are among my best friends, and these lazy summer afternoons on the front porch put a "bookmark in the frenzy" of mothering, harvesting, and homemaking. Peace may be a commodity in short supply, but the porch under the maples was steeped in it as another summer drew to a close.

• • •

I dropped my bags full of lima beans on the table in Mom's kitchen. I had brought two bucketfuls, thinking I could shell them while we talked.

Ida Mae studied the pile of limas, especially the ones with pods turned dry and brown. "I thought my lima beans were neglected this year because I had a new baby."

"My lima beans were neglected too," I replied. "But I don't know what was wrong, because I certainly didn't have a new baby."

"Perhaps you just hatched a new book," Mom suggested.

Her comment was greeted by laughter. "That's probably true," I admitted.

"Today the children may play in the watermelon field," Mom said a short time later. "The men are finished with it, so the children can pick all the little watermelons they want." She still felt badly about chasing them out earlier in the year.

The children were delighted with that announcement. In no time at all, Matthan, Melody, Makayla, Wesley, and KellyAnn were busy in the field behind the house. They followed the long rows all the way to the fencerow at the end of the property, and their faces grew warm and flushed, but they were having so much fun. Turned loose in the watermelon field, they picked the tiny latecomers that wouldn't grow any bigger and threw them at each other. The larger ones they broke open and slurped the pinkish centers, or threw them on the ground to make a glorious smash. And they made many trips to the porch, each time carrying a stash of little melons, from golf ball–sized and upward, that they wanted to keep. By the time the melon field lost its charms, we had some grubby children to clean up, but they were happy.

More melons had been smashed beneath the swing set, so we sent them to gather up the pieces. The swing set was full of children swooping back and forth on the swings. To add to the excitement, the older boys had taken the swings and notched the chains quite a bit higher off the ground. Matthan and Wesley and Makayla looked as if they were dangling in midair, but to them that was just dandy.

The older ones were making a train on the sliding board. KellyAnn sat at the bottom of the slide, and one by one the others slid down until the sliding board was full nearly to the top. Then the plastic began to buckle and they tumbled off the side, screeching and laughing, and collapsed in the grass.

In a cool and shady corner beside the porch, an elephant ear had grown to mammoth proportions. I had seen some pretty big ones, but never one so enormous as to stop you in your tracks and compel second and third glances.

"I've been having so much fun watching those leaves uncurl." Mom shook her head, laughing. "And now, would you look at it." The immense leaves had been carefully slit between each darker vein all the way up to the huge spine running down the center of the leaf. Green elephant ear flesh turning brown dangled there, limp and damaged.

"Oh no, who did that?" we asked, properly horrified. Not that we needed to ask. It looked exactly like the sort of job that would have been done by many busy little fingers.

To be sure, the children had made an amazing job of it. But it would grow again next year.

It was time for the children's long-looked-forward-to picnic before they headed back to school. Working together, we got a fire started in the fire ring, carried folding tables to the lawn, and assembled food and fixings. Emily put her baked beans on to heat and I located my bowl of potato salad in the fridge. Ida Mae was opening a few bags of snacks, with Steven in one arm. "I want jelly beans," Luella announced, walking past. "Mom, I want jelly beans."

"She must mean baked beans," I laughed.

"We need a few more hot dog sticks to go with the one I have," Mom said. "That one is like a little grill and makes six at a time, but we should have several."

"We brought our hot dog fork along," Amanda remembered. "It's still in the spring wagon. The boys could fetch it."

"Well, they already did," Mom replied with a laugh. "The boys have it out on the swing set. They fastened a box on the tines and are using it for a loudspeaker."

I went outside with an armful of picnic supplies to put on the tables. Sure enough, perched high on one of their ridiculously elevated swings was Wesley, auctioneering for all he was worth into the handle of the hot dog fork.

I handed the older boys a pack of hot dogs and the small handheld grill that would roast six at a time. "Here, why don't you get some hot dogs ready for us?"

They had several sticks of their own and were happy to help. Soon Lowell, Dean, Tristan, Travis, and Bradley were busy roasting the first hot dogs.

We scurried around finishing the final preparations, and the boys came in just as we were carrying the last items outside.

"It's time to eat, boys," Emily said. "Do you have some hot dogs ready?"

"Mmm, yes," the boys began.

"Well, good. We can fix the smallest children's plates first with those."

"But, Mom, we already ate the hot dogs we roasted," Tristan said.

"I guess that's all right too," Emily replied. "You can say your thank-you prayer for the ones in your stomach already."

The day was warm. Ice cubes kept the drinks cool, but the ice cream melted fast. It dripped off cones and onto sticky little hands. Sheba and the cats skulked around, shamelessly begging for handouts and eating everything that fell on the ground.

Amanda had baked cupcakes, and she held up one to show me. "Ah, Darla, did you notice my cupcakes?"

"Not really . . ." I pretended to groan. "Not those silicone papers again, and it's my turn to wash the dishes."

"Yes, that was the idea," Amanda said, pretending innocence.

"Oh well, it could be worse. At least we used paper plates today."

We sat on the porch for only a little bit after we finished eating. There were so many sticky hands and faces to wash, and ice cream to return to the freezer and food to take to the house. I filled the sink bowls with warm water and began washing dishes immediately. The sooner I started, the sooner I'd be finished.

After a while I realized that there were no cupcake papers mixed with the other dishes. That was suspicious. I dried my hands and went to the porch. Just a few bowls and dishes remained on the table. Everyone looked so innocent.

Alisha sat on a rocker reading a book. "Alisha, where are the cupcake papers?" I asked.

She stared at her book with great diligence. "Aw, Mom."

I looked from her to Jerelyn. "Come on, just tell me where you put them."

Alisha seemed distressed. "But, Mom, I'm not supposed to." I looked around the front yard, then jumped off the porch and headed for the spring wagon parked under the elm tree in front of the barn. It wouldn't hurt to check there.

Amanda came to the door. "That's not your wagon," she called. I kept on going. My suspicions proved correct. Under the seat I found a bag stuffed with all the dirty cupcake papers.

I carried the bag back to the house, victorious. "Jerelyn and Alisha tiptoed around gathering up every one of those," Regina told me. "Then they sneaked them out and hid them."

"All that hard work for nothing," Jerelyn complained.

Amanda had whispered instructions to the girls to gather up and hide them. "And I told Alisha and Jerelyn that if they told you they wouldn't be allowed to use my Big Shot anymore," Amanda said.

"Poor girls," I sympathized. "Well, they didn't tell me. I just found them."

I proceeded to wash the silicone cupcake wrappers. Before I was very far along I realized again why I don't like washing them.

We delayed homegoing as long as we could that final Tuesday, and even then the children were still begging for just a few more minutes, please, Mom, pretty, pretty, please.

But at last it was time to gather up our things, put the toys away, rescue David—who was celebrating the end of summer by splashing in the toilet—and coax reluctant children out the door.

Their goodbyes were just a little pouty, it being the last Tuesday of summer, and just a little sad. That they were excited about school starting did not automatically mean they were eager to say farewell to their beloved Tuesdays at Mom's house, and next summer was still a long way off.

"Say goodbye to Wesley," I told Matthan as we left. "Next Tuesday when he's playing here you will be in school."

The two boys stared at each other. Neither of them said anything for a little while.

"Goodbye, Wesley," said Matthan at last, sounding subdued.

"Goodbye, Matthan," said Wesley, just as soberly.

And summer was already over, gone by too fast.

• • •

*"Now is the accepted time; behold, now is the day
of salvation."*

2 CORINTHIANS 6:2

SEPTEMBER

Babyhood Vanishes When First Grade Starts

ALTHOUGH THE CALENDARS insist that, officially, summer continues another month, for me it's over when the children go back to school.

I biked alone through the silent, tree-lined road that first Tuesday morning in September. There was no chatter to fill the quiet morning air as I threaded my way out to the blacktop road, for Matthan had gone to school with Alisha.

This morning no little boy pedaled beside me. No little boy was chattering and asking brain-boggling questions such as "Could a gnat drown in a tear?" and "What do those germs want inside me anyhow?" No little boy to make me laugh.

I thought back across all the years that had slipped away too fast. This summer, as never quite before, I'd been forced to face the fact that my children were growing up faster than I liked, and even without my permission. While Cody was at work, the teepee in the woods fell down, and the Native American campground that he and the little boys (Matthan and their cousin) had made the previous year was silent and deserted. No one played there any more. Alisha had set up her playhouse again, but more often than not, no one played there either.

She had other things to do, and the small furniture stood idly, collecting dirt.

And when Cody went to the store to buy a pair of shoes, he came home with elevens. What's more, they were the right size. Those were not the feet that fit so snug into the palm of my hand when I helped them begin to walk, just the day before yesterday or so.

Now even Matthan had grown up and gone to school. The last lingering bits of babyhood always vanish forever in that first-grade aura.

Lines of a verse from Jeremiah teased the edges of my memory, something about summer being past before we're ready. I tried to recall it. "The harvest is past, the summer is ended, and we are not saved" (Jeremiah 8:20).

I pedaled faster and tried to think of a cheerier verse, considering that I felt sad enough already. Something like "Sing unto the Lord a new song," from Psalm 96. "Sing unto the Lord, all the earth. Sing unto the Lord, bless his name . . ."

• • •

The screen door on the front porch was stuck when I arrived. I pulled at it again. It remained jammed at the top of the door frame. "Kick at the bottom of it," Mom called.

I did so, and the door popped open. "Oh, I see. And here I thought you had latched it shut on the inside to keep me out."

"Now why would we do that?" Mom asked. "Because you looked so old, coming up the hill without any children along?"

"We decided you looked almost like a grandma," Regina agreed. "With all your children in school now."

They were all smiling, so I started smiling too. So wonderful is the consolation of sisterly sympathy that I cheered right up. Even if my children are growing up too fast, here are my sisters, growing old, or at least middle-aged, right along with me. The years are passing one by one, a little like the shadows that slip across the mountains each afternoon, but we are sisters still. Even the surprises that the years often bring can't change that.

Decades ago, when we all still had the same last name, we were sisters by chance of birth and took for granted the bonds of our heritage. Today we are friends by choice as much as we are sisters, and we feel amazingly blessed to have grown from these roots. It's not something to take for granted anymore.

• • •

Mom's kitchen seemed to have enlarged quite a lot in one week's time, for ten children had gone back to school. Five little ones remained—Wesley, Makayla, Corey, Janessa, and Luella—besides the three babies. We would have space in which to work, and enough silence to hear each other talk.

But before we had quite settled down to our forenoon together, the children were running out onto the porch and back into the kitchen. As they ran they held one hand over their cheeks and yelled. "I've been stung!" they were screaming. "Ow! Ow! I've been stung."

Their screaming was punctuated by many giggles, so we knew they were only playing. When we got tired of their noise they were shooed to the porch. "It's just a handful of children to make such a racket," Amanda remarked, closing the door behind them.

"Maybe they feel they have to raise a fuss," Mom suggested, "to make up for all the ones who aren't here anymore."

Soon they were happy and busy outside, completely absorbed in quiet play. The only times we heard them were when Corey and Makayla came inside and asked for large tumblers. These they filled with water. "We're making soup," they explained, and they returned repeatedly, asking for refills. The tumblers and their little hands became muddier and dirtier each time. Grass clippings and bits of soil clung to the beads of moisture on the sides of the tumblers.

Quite a while later Amanda went to the packing shed to collect some produce. She came back to the house with a pile of red, yellow, and orange peppers in a box. "I brought some along for you, if you want them," she said, tilting the box under my nose.

"Indeed I do," I said, putting the peppers into my bag. "Thanks. I just made some dip that will go well with these."

Amanda wasn't listening. She stepped closer and spoke in a lowered tone. "And there's some amazing succulent soup outside too."

I didn't understand. "Succulent soup?"

"Yes, you know, that soup the children were making? They made it out of Mom's succulents."

I followed her outside, and soon our other sisters came too. It really was soup. The children had mixed it on the front walk just off the porch, and it overflowed into a shallow depression in the nearby lawn. It was made of mud and grass and succulent leaves. Lots of succulent leaves.

"Oh no," Ida Mae sighed. "This is what happens when we don't check up on them more often."

"But where did all these succulents come from?" Regina asked.

"I couldn't find too much damage yet," Amanda said. "But maybe I missed something."

We sneaked around checking on all the potted succulents until Mom became curious. "Whatever are you doing?"

"Ah, that soup," my sheepish sisters explained. "Do you see what it's made of? The main ingredient is succulents."

There were some advantages after all, I realized, to having Matthan in school.

We finally discovered where most of the leaves came from: the planters beside the front walk were heavily scalped.

"Don't worry about it," Mom said. "I planned to scalp them myself when I move them to the greenhouse before frost. That's how I start new plants."

• • •

The high, almost musical whine of the corn harvester in the distance marked the changing of the seasons as surely as school's beginning. The men worked together in various fields and farms, making silage piles and filling silos. The harvester sang the tune of autumn in the background.

• • •

As we sat in Mom's kitchen, I'd hear the other children call "Mom!" in a variety of tones, and I would look up, only to remember that Matthan was in school and someone else was the mom in demand.

"At home I've started talking to the animals now that Matthan's in school," I told Wesley, and he responded by giving me a disbelieving glance.

But it's true. In the house I talk to Matthan's four gossipy parakeets. When I'm outside I can carry on a reasonably interesting conversation with Alisha's cats. And if any of the horses are in the pasture when I'm hanging up laundry, I even talk to them.

"But there are compensations," I admitted to my sisters, who looked as if they were trying to decide whether to sympathize. "After I manage to help everyone out the door each morning I get to sit down and catch my breath. Then I have my breakfast with coffee while reading a book."

"I guess it will be six years before I can do that," Ida Mae said, rocking Steven, who was wearing a blue puppy sleeper and looking very cuddly indeed.

"Wesley, maybe I could take you along home sometimes," I suggested. "You could be my little boy for a little while."

Wesley gave me that trademark grin—part mischief, part innocence—and didn't reply. He knew I was teasing.

"Maybe we could share," Emily offered kindly. "You could have him one week, and I could have him the next." But we knew she was also teasing.

"Then you would also not have any children at home anymore," Mom told Emily, looking as if she found it hard to believe that these were her daughters she was talking about, and when had they aged so fast?

"Do you want the girls too?" Amanda asked.

"Sure, why not?" I agreed. "Bring them to me sometimes."

"Maybe you would like to have Steven too," Ida Mae said. "You could start a mini daycare center."

"Think about all the stories you would soon be able to write," Amanda added.

• • •

Arlie the neighbor woman had delivered a basketful of painted rocks for Amanda's girls, and we all took turns admiring them. The rocks, smooth and round or oval, were each painted to look like an animal. There was a little fawn, a raccoon, a fox, a deer mouse, and assorted other animals in various shapes and colors. A few tiny ones in the bottom of the basket were painted as ladybugs. It was an adorable collection.

"Wouldn't Matthan like these," I remarked looking through the basket. "Maybe I could ask Arlie to paint some for him."

So that's why I was at the bottom of the hill where a load of creek gravel had been dumped not too long before. As I sorted through the rocks, selecting only the ones that were smooth and the right shape, I reflected that a basketful of rocks sounded like a strange idea for a Christmas present. But Matthan often played with small stones, and he loved animals of all kinds. I could just imagine him spending hours with those little stone "animals."

• • •

A wagon rattled down the gravel lane to the pepper field, and Emily went to peer out the window. "Wesley and Makayla have just hitched a ride to the produce field," she told Amanda. "It's a good thing I checked when I did, or we wouldn't have known where they disappeared to." She shook out a plastic bag. "And now I've just remembered that I had better go look for some seconds of peppers when the men unload the buckets at the packing shed. I want to make pizza sauce tomorrow."

"I was thinking about making a batch of pepper relish to can," Ida Mae said. "But I talked myself out of it again."

"Why did you do that?" Amanda asked. "Pepper relish is our favorite kind. I should make more of it."

"It's easy for me to talk myself out of canning sometimes," Emily said. "But I really do have to make pizza sauce yet this year."

"I enjoy canning relishes and things like that," Ida Mae said. "It's just that I wasn't sure when I would find time to do it."

• • •

Corey and Wesley talked almost nonstop all during dinner. Maybe they were glad for a chance to be heard. It was their turn to keep the conversational ball rolling now that all the older children were in school. They did a good job of it.

"And Corey can tell the most remarkable stories," Mom said with a smile. "I still remember the day he came into the kitchen and told me a long and interesting tale about the horse sale he attended with his daddy one weekend. It took a long time until I realized he hadn't actually been to a horse sale; he was just making up a story to entertain me."

"He does a lot of that," Regina agreed. "He's got a big imagination."

I was sampling the dessert Emily had brought. It had a cream cheese center. "What did you use to make the bottom crust?" I asked. "And what's on top? Brownies?"

"Yes, I used some of those surplus brownies," Emily admitted. "I bought too many at the Denver Foods place, and the boys were tired of them. So I cut the sprinkles off the top and used the brownie part to make this dessert."

"It's good," I said. "I like it."

"You really weren't supposed to ask what I used to make this," Emily continued. "Wasn't it just last week that Mom was blaming us for using Tuesdays to get rid of food we no longer want?

"Yes, like those jalapeno cheese squares that are still in my freezer," Mom spoke up. "But you all know I was only teasing."

"About this coffee pudding I made"—Ida Mae spoke up—"I used up some milk that was starting to taste slightly sour."

"The coffee pudding is really good, though," I told Ida Mae. It was smooth and creamy and richly flavored with coffee. "I need to copy the recipe and make some too."

COFFEE PUDDING

6 cups cold milk, separated
1 cup sugar
3 tablespoons instant coffee
¾ cup Thermflo or Clearjel
1 tablespoon butter
1 tablespoon vanilla
8 ounces whipped topping
Oreo cookie crumbs (optional)
Banana slices (optional)

In a large saucepan, mix and heat 5 cups milk, sugar, and instant coffee. Separately, combine remaining 1 cup milk with Thermflo or Clearjel. Stir into hot mixture, and bring to a boil. Remove from heat and add butter and vanilla. Allow to cool. Fold in whipped topping. Garnish with Oreo cookie crumbs and bananas (optional).

• • •

There came an afternoon of Hurricane Irma rain, dripping off the leaves and sliding off the roof in long silver drops. It cocooned us into our own remote little world that was cozy and comfortable and far removed from the devastation the hurricane had caused farther south when it reached land. I read the paper that Christopher had left in the kitchen, looked at the pictures, tried to imagine the loss so many people were facing, and wished there were more we could do to help them.

One concern I had at the moment was that if the rain kept up, I would have to borrow a raincoat to bike home, plus a large bag to keep my box of things dry. I thought about it off and on while browsing through the latest issue of *Keepers at Home*, stalling on my self-appointed task of cutting out two more dresses for Alisha.

At last I flipped the piece of fabric open across the table. "This house is so littered with card-making supplies," I complained, moving aside partly colored stamped pictures, pencil boxes crammed with colored pencils and markers, scissors, a pencil sharpener, and more.

A shopping bag holding a stack of Amanda's latest finished cards made me pause to look through them. "But if you can make cards like this," I conceded, "it would be a shame not to."

Amanda looked up. "Yes, don't you think that would be a lot more fun than writing another book?"

"Oh, no, not even close," I replied, hastily returning her cards to the bag. "I'm trying hard to finish some of my other work so I'm allowed to start a new one."

Several groans were my only reply.

Sewing was one of those tasks I was trying to finish. I rummaged through my pile of things for Alisha's dress pattern. "Sewing wouldn't be so bad if I once again had a pattern that actually fit like it's supposed to."

"Have you tried the one you used here at home when you were girls?" Mom asked.

"I don't believe I have," I replied. "I'm going to try the one I borrowed from the neighbors again. If I use it often enough maybe I'll learn where to cut differently to personalize it, and it'll fit better."

"Let me clean out my pattern drawer," Mom offered. "Maybe I can find the dress pattern you girls used when you were still at home."

Moments of laughter followed as we explored the contents of a long-neglected drawer. "I really can't believe I saved this," Mom commented, holding up an oddly shaped piece of wooden spindle. "Do any of you know what it is?"

We didn't, so she showed us. It was a broken part from one of the chairs at the table. "I must have meant to fix it sometime," Mom said, "and it never happened. But I wonder why. The spindle was already broken."

For some reason this struck us as funny, and we laughed hysterically.

An odd assortment of other things appeared, along with old patterns now slated for the trash. A crumpled construction-paper girl from an old classmate was unearthed, a broken toy or two that made us exclaim, "I remember that!," doll accessories, and a stack of bookmarks. Amanda sorted through the stack. "May I have some of these?" she asked Mom.

"Of course," Mom replied. "I'm sure I don't want that many."

"When you're finished I would also look through them," Ida Mae told Amanda.

"Books are very magic," Amanda read from a bookmark she was holding.

Our old dress pattern surfaced at last, and it was time to stop laughing and reminiscing and get busy. Those dresses for Alisha weren't going to sew themselves, much as I wished they would.

• • •

Amanda had ordered a different Big Shot, in a new and larger model, and now that it had arrived she brought her used one along for Alisha. "And I've also filled a bag of my dies that she may borrow for a while," she said, fishing it out of her box.

I took it, feeling out of my element. I couldn't believe I was having to learn all this stuff whether I wanted to or not. "Anyway, this thing is too big for me to put in my bike box," I said, parking it on the other side of the room. "I'll pick it up some other time."

"If Alisha finds out it's here you may be picking it up pretty soon," Regina commented.

"In fact, you may find yourself biking down to fetch it later on tonight yet," Amanda teased.

"Oh, no I won't," I replied with believable conviction. Alisha had waited this long for a Big Shot of her own, and she could wait a little longer.

The rain kept dripping and we kept talking. The conversation ranged from topics such as Charles Dickens and his books to whether it was normal or unnecessary to have reading material in the bathroom. We formed two opinions on that, between the ones who kept some books or magazines there, and the ones who deemed it completely unnecessary.

We were more in agreement about Charles Dickens, because none of us cared much for his books. Here we disagreed with our brother, who bought and read each one he could find and found them interesting rather than long-winded.

Ida Mae left early to take Bradley and Melody to their dentist appointments, and Luella stayed at Mom's house. She would go home with Regina later on, running across the fields and along the lane with Corey, to play there until her daddy came to bring her home.

But at the moment Luella felt a little lost, and that was why she decided to go look for Corey and Wesley, who were playing in the packing shed while the men readied produce for the next day's auction.

She was gone a short while, and then came trudging back to the house, crying as if her heart were broken. "Corey and Wesley went on the wagon," she wailed between sobs, in answer to our questions.

Apparently the wagon had departed for the field to haul more buckets of produce to the shed, and Luella had been just in time to see the two lucky boys who got to ride along—while missing it herself. No wonder she was crying.

"Would you like to play with my paper bird?" Mom asked. "I made this thing from a pattern in a book. Do you see its wings? Now, to make it fly we slip a penny into the slot between its wings, and it's supposed to soar—"

The bird crashed on its beak instead. "Now that's not really flying," Mom objected. "Let's try again, shall we, Luella?"

The hapless bird took several more nosedives as it bumbled around the kitchen, and Luella lifted up her voice and wept loudly, perhaps in sympathy for the clumsy bird.

"Luella, I think I know what you need." Emily picked her up and carried her to the pantry shelves. "Chocolate chips!"

Luella's tears stopped. She sat on Emily's lap at the table and munched her way through a splendid pile of chocolate chips.

"Did the chocolate chips make it better?" Emily asked after a while. Luella beamed through the last traces of her tears.

"Chocolate chips make many things better, don't they?" I asked.

"Now do you want some pretzels?" Emily inquired.

Luella agreed, and the little snack did the trick. Soon she and Emily were both coloring, and Luella had forgotten about her missed ride to the produce field.

All too soon it was time for me to leave if I wanted to arrive home before the children returned from school. And I did. I was still a mother.

Sisters must stick together when they can, and none of us would be willing to disband our weekly gatherings. After more than fifteen years of Tuesdays they are woven into the very fabric of our lives. But they are merely one dimension of life, a part that adds meaning and purpose to all our other relationships. Another part of life waited for each of us at our homes, and now it was time to go back to being wives, moms, homemakers. Next Tuesday we would return to Mom's house. Here at our old home we would once again be sisters, daughters, friends. There was a timelessness to this legacy of family, in all its seasons, an abiding security. Things change and times change, but family goes on through the ups and downs, through spring's sunshine and winter's cold alike.

One more month had vanished. The ebb and flow of the seasons carried us always onward.

• • •

"Watch ye, stand fast in the faith."

1 CORINTHIANS 16:13

OCTOBER

Coffee High, Cat Tails, and Snapping Turtles

DEW-SOAKED GRASS and puddles of fog deep in the valleys marked the relentless cadence of the seasons. The light was different too.

It slanted in long swords through the trees, amber and golden. The shadows were deeper.

Delayed by rain, the silo-filling at the farm was pushed into October. That was why the first Tuesday of the month found us bustling around the kitchen, helping (or perhaps hindering?) Mom as we worked together to make dinner for the men who were busy with the annual silage-making day.

The harvester's song was closer at hand today, and more urgent. Our hands flew, keeping time to its rhythm. I sliced new red potatoes into wedges, to be baked with butter and seasonings. Regina washed and chopped Chinese cabbage for a salad; Mom was readying green beans to barbecue. There were meatballs to place in a pan, rolls to heat, and all the salad fixings to prepare.

"I wonder how much of this salad I should make for dinner today?" Regina asked. "At home I chop up three leaves and that's enough. Most of the children don't care for it."

"I like Chinese cabbage salad," I answered, watching her add diced hard-boiled eggs while Emily fried the bacon. "But I seldom make it either. No one else wants to help me eat it."

Emily flipped the bacon and it sizzled with renewed vigor. Mom mixed a ketchup-and-brown-sugar sauce for the beans, and Amanda laid down one of the new fall book catalogs through which she had been paging. "Should I be helping you with anything?"

"No, you shouldn't," I replied firmly, washing more potatoes. "We've got enough people working in the kitchen already."

"We're all but stepping on each other here," Mom agreed.

Emily forked through the strips of bacon that were spitting bubbles of hot grease. "I think I could be convinced to do something else."

"I brought along some stamped pictures to color," Regina said, whipping together the dressing for the salad. "I'd be glad to go do that."

But they kept right on with what they were doing. It wouldn't do for dinner to be late today.

• • •

While we were working at the sink we were interrupted by Luella's terrified screams. They came from somewhere in the front yard, and we all rushed outside to investigate.

Jerelyn reached Luella first and picked her up. "It's a tail," Luella shrieked, clinging to Jerelyn.

"What? What is it?" we demanded.

"A turtle," Janessa explained, pointing.

An ugly, gray-shelled turtle was indeed creeping through the grass close to the porch, head extended and tail outstretched. Luella was stiff with fright.

"Why, that's a snapping turtle," Amanda exclaimed, taking a closer look.

"Are you sure?" I asked doubtfully. Did they venture so far from water?

"Oh, I'm sure. Years ago I used to help our brothers catch them at the creek. It's small, but it's certainly a snapping turtle."

The cat and her kitten were inching in stiff-legged circles around the turtle. When they came too close the turtle hissed, and the cats leaped backward, tails fluffed.

"We'd better keep that kitten from getting too close," I said. I had visions of the turtle snapping up a kitten leg for lunch, of half a dozen screeching children, and of some screaming moms as well. "The turtle may try to bite it."

"I'll hold her," Wesley volunteered. He dove in to rescue the kitten, and it scrammed in one direction while its mom sailed in another. Wesley chased the kitten a long way before he caught up with it behind the house, and then he carried it back to the porch.

"Let me find a shovel," Mom said, after we had all stood around the turtle and made an appropriate fuss about the sheer ugliness of the creature. "I'll scoop it up and carry it back to the field."

Corey stood on the trampoline, well out of the way and looking terrified. He watched the proceedings with wide eyes and open mouth.

The turtle didn't think much of Mom's plan to remove it and protested in every reptilian way it knew. But at last all the ugly gray length of it was on the shovel, and Mom hurried back to the field with it, shovel held at arm's length. "I certainly hope the thing won't decide to crawl along the handle of the shovel," she said. "I don't know what would happen if it came charging up at me."

With the turtle out of the way, and the grass once more safe for the children to play in, we returned to our work. When the excitement was over, Corey trotted indoors holding his nose between finger and thumb. "Phew, it stinks!" he complained. "I smelled that bad snapper turtle smell."

• • •

The children were outside watching the horses and wagons as they trundled in from the cornfields with loads of chopped corn, blew the silage up into the silo by way of the blower, and headed back out. We popped pans into the oven and put kettles of food on the stove to heat, then turned our attention to the desserts, two of which were made of apples.

"Apple crisp and apple cake," I announced, pulling the top off a last pan and peering at its contents. "And can you believe this," I added, holding up a chocolate cupcake. "Amanda used silicone cupcake papers again. And—oh good—I'm not washing dishes today."

"I think it's my turn to do the dishes," Regina said, turning to look at the cupcake I was holding. "I don't know if I can wash those things."

"This time," Amanda informed her, "I'm going to hide them and you'll never find them."

And so she did.

• • •

"I tried your coffee pudding recipe last week," I told Ida Mae. "All day long I was looking forward to eating some of that delicious pudding for supper. And then," I said with a sigh, "I took the bowl out of the fridge and it was so solid it could have been cut with a knife and lifted out in slabs. Mud-colored slabs at that."

Everyone looked as sympathetic as they could manage, in between laughing.

"I tried to stir in the whipped cream," I added, "but it was more like smashing it in. Then we had slimy lumps of muddy hash in whipped cream. It was awful. We ended up giving it to Alisha's cats."

"They likely got a coffee high from that," Emily suggested.

• • •

Wesley and Makayla and Corey came inside asking for food. "We are so hungry," they insisted.

We looked at the clock and persuaded them to wait a little. "Dinner is almost ready. Then you can eat."

"But our bellies are so empty," Wesley protested.

"My belly has nothing left in it," Corey agreed, trying to look tragic but failing because of his big grin.

Makayla rummaged through a drawer and found a coloring book and crayons. "Let's do this until dinner is ready," she suggested, and they all lay down on the floor on their stomachs and scribbled contentedly.

• • •

It was so warm and balmy, with showers of leaves separating from the trees at intervals, that I sat outside on the porch to rock Steven. Luella and Janessa were there too. They were sitting on the porch steps playing with a doll, and their "doll" happened to be the kitten everyone played with on Tuesdays but no one named. They smiled and whispered and smiled some more. They were in church with their "baby" and it was behaving beautifully and purring with all its might.

The church services were interrupted when Corey and Wesley set up an auction behind them. Wesley sold the acorn squash he found on the porch to Corey, the single bidder.

And Steven opened his eyes wide and gazed with wonderment at them all.

• • •

Dinnertime, with the table stretched long enough to also seat all the men who were filling the silo, was over at last. Regina washed a huge pile of dishes, and then we were ready to prop up our feet awhile. There were pictures to color and magazines to read, as well as stamping to do.

Occasionally we discussed the situation with North Korea, remarked upon Donald Trump's presidency, mentioned things in the news like the tragic shooting in Las Vegas. Sometimes I read various newspapers to learn more about the world around me.

But sometimes the more I learned, the less I wished to learn. Those were the times I realized that I was happiest simply being a country homemaker, with a family to care for, a garden to tend, and sisters to share life with. Those are the things that, in the end, give real meaning to my life.

"For there is no friend like a sister / In calm or stormy weather," wrote poet Christina Georgina Rosetti a long time ago. But it's still true today.

The October afternoons drifted idly by in this fashion as we talked about things sisters find enthralling, and laughed about things only sisters find amusing. At Mom's house we've learned to treasure life, for it is very short, and to embrace the blissful ordinariness of ordinary days. In the end, those are the best days of all.

• • •

"I have to copy Alisha's Bible verse yet, for their memory class at school this week," I announced to no one in particular. "Then I'll get to sit down too."

"Why would you still have to copy Alisha's Bible verses for her?" Ida Mae asked in surprise.

"Well, it's this way," I explained. "Their verse is in German this week, and it's from the Old Testament. When she wanted to copy it last night we discovered that we have only the New Testament in German. All our Bibles with the Old Testament included are in English."

So today I took Dad's large, worn German Bible from the shelf to copy Isaiah 41:10. "Fürchte dich nicht, ich bin mit dir; weiche nicht, denn ich bin dein Gott; ich stärke dich, ich helfe dir auch, ich erhalte dich durch die rechte Hand meiner Gerechtigkeit."

Isaiah 41:10 has long been a favorite verse of mine— although those are subject to frequent change with the seasons of life—and in German the words had a victorious sort of rhythm. It would be a good verse, I decided, for me to memorize in German as well as English.

• • •

David was sitting on Regina's lap while she worked at coloring the next batch of pictures for her cards. Corey sat beside her, happy to combine all the shades of green as he colored a rose. It was the first green rose I ever saw, but he was satisfied. "Don't put anything on my card," he warned when I came too close.

Makayla's fifth birthday had just come and gone, and Mom had given her a doll, complete with a homemade outfit. Since the day ten years ago when Jerelyn turned five, each granddaughter has received one of those keepsake dolls on her fifth birthday.

"Makayla," Mom said today, "what did you name your birthday doll?"

Makayla stopped coloring and began to smile. But for some reason she was too shy to tell us the name of her new doll.

"What did you name her?" Amanda asked. "I forgot."

Makayla came to whisper into Amanda's ear, and then they were both smiling. "Now tell Grandma," Amanda urged.

Makayla was still shy. She ran across the room to whisper into Mom's ear. Mom looked a little bewildered as she listened.

"May we know too, Makayla?" we asked.

Yes, Makayla thought we would be allowed to know what she had named her new doll. There was only one problem. She didn't want to tell us.

"Tell me," Janessa offered, "and I'll tell them."

So Makayla sat down on the couch beside Janessa and whispered into her ear. Janessa just looked baffled. "What?"

It took Makayla several more tries. At last Janessa's brown eyes lit up. "Makayla!" she announced.

Makayla's smile covered her entire face. "Yes! I named her Makayla too."

"That is a pretty name," we assured her, smiling too. "And you will never forget it."

• • •

The October mornings continued cool and frosty. Leaves swooped earthward in great drifts, especially when it was rainy or windy. There was a crunchy brown carpet on the gravel road where I biked and a coppery golden glow of leaves over my head.

One morning a cold rain fell, and I thought about staying home. But Tuesday always calls to be spent at Mom's house, so I bundled up, pulled on a raincoat and warm boots, and went.

Charlotte stayed home warm and dry in the barn. She and I didn't mix so well with all the combines and tractors roaring in the corn and soybean fields just then. Of course, if they stayed in the fields we wouldn't have a problem. But the monsters rumble on the roads sometimes, between farms and fields, and Charlotte thinks they'd like to gobble her along with the crops. So my bike and I got along better through October.

The mornings might be cool and sometimes rainy, but the afternoons all that month were sunny and warm. The year was going out with a gentle smile, full of serene acceptance and the wisdom of age.

Arlie had Matthan's basketful of painted rock animals ready. It was waiting on Mom's table, with all those baby animal faces looking up. "Aren't they cute?" Amanda said, lifting out a fawn, a tiny coon, a little gray field mouse. A strange expression appeared on her face. She jerked away her hand and piled the rocks back into the basket.

"Ah, I see."

"What?" I peered into the basket, puzzled by her reaction. A smooth round stone under the bunny was coiled in red and black and yellow stripes, its head lifted. At least, it was painted so that it appeared so. "Eek," I said. "I see too."

Ida Mae came to peer over my shoulder. "Does Arlie know how much Matthan likes snakes?"

"I don't see how she could," I replied. Deciding to be brave, I looked through the rocks, all the way to the bottom of the basket where cute little ladybug and turtle rocks hid. "But it's just what Matthan will like, so I'll tolerate the snake."

• • •

There was a gallon of honey waiting for me, harvested from the beehives Christopher tended on the farm. Its golden-amber weight dragged on my arms as I carried it to my box, then dug out dollars to pay for it.

The daily Bible calendar held a new verse for Tuesday, one from Job 34:32, which I'd never taken particular notice of before. "That which I see not teach thou me."

It was a good thought, I decided. A teachable heart, open to God's will and guidance, was necessary if I wanted to continue to always learn more about serving my Savior and King more devotedly.

• • •

Wesley, Makayla, and Luella were sitting side by side in Mom's recliner. They had a pile of books on their laps and were telling each other stories about the pictures. I observed them and thought, We do start them young in this book mania.

David toddled along the row of cabinets in the kitchen. He opened drawers and removed items, opened doors and cleaned off shelves. And while noise and chatter flowed around her, Ashley sat on a blanket on the floor and played with toys. She sat there contented and amused for an hour. We timed her and were amazed.

"She is a happy baby," Amanda said, "but even she doesn't do that at home. She just likes Tuesdays."

We indicated that we found this amusing. "No, it's true," Amanda insisted. "She likes all the commotion, the coming and going, and everything that's happening around her. She's entertained."

I worked at mending a pair of Matthan's school pants and recalled how he'd been trying to explain something about his cousins to Alisha one day. Alisha didn't understand whom he meant, and said so. "I mean the Tuesday people," Matthan cried, frustrated.

It's true, we all thrive on our Tuesdays together. The grandchildren have, on occasion, even called Mom "Grandma Tuesday," which she said made her feel as if she were on a plantation in the South before the Civil War. I suppose, as Matthan says, we're Tuesday folks.

• • •

Regina and Emily were working on pants too, school pants for their boys, and the children were no longer looking at picture books. Perhaps inspired by David's explorations, they were playing under the open drawers in the kitchen cabinets. This was their ship now, declared Wesley, Corey, and Makayla, and they were sailing to far-off ports. It took a great deal of noise, however, to furnish and move their ship and sail it off. We tolerated it, but only for a while.

"You are being very loud," Mom remarked above the noise.

We agreed. Our heads were ringing with the racket issuing from the "ship."

"We should get their coats and chase them outside for a while," their moms decided.

The children liked the idea. They ran for their coats and skipped outside. Soon they were romping through the fallen leaves, scattering them far and wide while they yelled at the top of their exceedingly healthy lungs.

"Mom, did you mention having extra bluing?" Amanda asked. "I'm not sure where to buy it."

"Bluing?" I perked up my ears. "I've been wanting some too."

"Me too," Ida Mae added. "And I didn't know where to get it."

"I bought two bottles by mistake, when what I really needed was something else." Mom found both bottles on her closet shelves. "You can have these. But why the sudden need for bluing?"

"Coal gardens," I explained.

"Coal gardens," Ida Mae and Amanda agreed.

"I don't know where to find coals," I continued. "But I'll manage somehow. I promised the children we'd make a coal garden this winter, and that they could have one to take to school."

"And bluing is the hardest ingredient of all to find," Ida Mae said.

"Well, here it is," Mom told us. "I guess that was a lucky mistake."

Coal gardens are fascinating for children and adults alike, and they're easy to make. Finding the ingredients is the biggest difficulty. You mix together six tablespoons each of bluing, water, and salt, along with one tablespoon ammonia, and pour it over a dozen coals in a deep dish or a small fishbowl. Save any extra liquid. Add food color, and watch the garden grow. To keep it growing, carefully add more of the liquid at the side. It forms some astonishing growths.

• • •

A generous crop of sweet potatoes had been dug and stored for winter. "Could we make spicy sweet potato cubes for dinner?" Emily asked. "I'm hungry for some."

"Of course," Mom replied. "I'll bring some sweet potatoes up from the cellar."

Emily washed and peeled the sweet potatoes and diced each one. We dropped the small cubes into a plastic bag and drizzled them with cooking oil. We added brown sugar, salt, chili powder, and just enough cayenne pepper to give the cubes a slightly tangy flavor. After closing the bag and giving it a good shaking to spread the seasonings around, we poured the cubes on a cookie sheet and baked them for about an hour at 375 degrees.

I also love to eat sweet potatoes prepared this way, but the children weren't convinced. Janessa eyed the lone cube on her plate and finally braved the oddity. She chewed, shuddered, and grimaced. The sweet potato was swallowed at last with a big bite of bread and jelly. Janessa looked relieved.

"Mom," she said to Amanda, "I never want to eat something like that again."

• • •

My sisters and I can never agree about whether stamp art or writing is more fun. Despite the many times we return to the matter, we still manage to be good natured about it. And these differences, however minor, keep life interesting. We must agree to disagree about it, because they have no intention of taking up writing, and I have no intention of taking up card-making. It's anyone's guess as to who will capitulate first.

The subject came up again today after dinner. Regina was shortening the table. Amanda was drying the dishes. Soon both jobs were neglected. The table gaped open missing boards, the dishes dripped in the drainer. Regina and Amanda had their heads together over a stamper catalog, discussing which ones to buy next, which colors complemented which card, and whatever else it is they find so enthralling.

Ida Mae stopped washing dishes to gaze at them. "Do you suppose there's such a thing as stamper ADD?"

"There must be," I replied. "It's what they have." I rubbed my forehead and added, "I've had a headache all day. Do you suppose it's because I didn't have any coffee this morning?"

"It's possible," Emily said. "If you're used to drinking some each morning."

"At least we don't get a headache from being addicted to stamping," Regina said, returning to her work. "Like caffeine withdrawal or something."

"Maybe not," I said doubtfully. "But perhaps you would get shakes and tremors if you couldn't stamp for too long."

"Yes, and my hand would just start coloring in the air," Regina added, demonstrating.

"My head aches too," Amanda said, beginning to wipe the dishes again. "I haven't done any stamping the last several days. Do you suppose it's stamping withdrawal?"

We finished the dishes with laughter. We were girls together, years ago in a time that seems increasingly far away, and that was good. Today we are women together, and that's even better.

There is a lot of dailiness to our lives, a lot that's ordinary. But in the midst of everyday living we find a lot of satisfaction. It's in families cared for, jobs well done, chores completed. In the color and creativity that each new day holds, no matter how ordinary. The special moments shared with laughter and chatter, over food or crayons or words, as the case may be. And the kitchen at Mom's house keeps us connected.

No matter how ordinary our lives are, we like to share the details. Sisters are some of God's best gifts, a happy reason not to go life solo.

• • •

Fall brings an abundance of book catalogs from Amish and Mennonite bookstores all over the eastern United States. Everyone is getting ready for those long winter evenings. Mom was searching for a few certain titles to complete various series for her library. The rest of us were searching for new titles, or simply browsing.

I mentioned a certain prolific author as I paged through the latest catalog. "She doesn't seem to have a new book out this year," I noted. "That's unusual."

"She must have decided to do something more interesting and worthwhile with her life," Emily suggested.

"Yes," Regina agreed. "I'm pretty sure she has started stamping cards instead."

"I really should make a congratulations card for her," Emily went on, trying to look serious. "I'd add a letter and say that I heard she's stopped writing books and is doing something exciting for a change."

"If you actually want to do that," I said, laughing, "I'll find her address for you."

We sorted through a huge stack of unused cards from a flea market. They were birthday cards and valentines, most saying "To my wife" in various forms, and we discussed this idea. Did we, or did we not, want to choose some of our favorites and take them home and give them to our husbands? "Here," we would say, "are some cards that I wanted. Would you please give them to me on my birthday and on Valentine's Day?"

The idea was discarded at last, reluctantly but with much laughter, because a few of my sisters admitted that they really would have to decorate, and further embellish with stamp art and stickers, the not-nearly-nice-enough center designs.

And then, in a garden magazine several decades old, Regina discovered an article about babying one's houseplants, and she read parts of it to us.

The author recommended using an old baby stroller to move one's houseplants. Such as wheeling them inside at night when the temperatures dropped and then moving them outside again the following day. She also advised cooing to them and singing a few lullabies. It wouldn't do the plants any good, of course, but it would be sure to drive the neighbors crazy.

When we finally stopped chuckling, we discussed the possibilities. "What if I did put a houseplant in the stroller and walked out the lane with it?" Emily asked. "Singing a lullaby as I went? What would the neighbors say?"

"I'd pretend I didn't know you," Amanda assured her.

"That's what you can do next year when Wesley goes to school," I suggested. "Take a plant for a walk to the mailbox every day."

"I'll tell my girls to start praying for a baby for you instead," Amanda offered. "They wanted to start praying for a baby again. I asked them to hold on a little yet." She waited until we stopped laughing to add, "Of course, their idea was to pray for a little boy this time."

"But if they want to start praying for a baby for Emily," Mom said, "they should pray for a little girl, don't you think?"

Ashley found this conversation very funny indeed. She smiled and smiled. It was evident that she approved.

• • •

"The Lord thy God, he is God, the faithful God, which keepeth covenant and mercy with them that love him and keep his commandments to a thousand generations."

DEUTERONOMY 7:9

NOVEMBER

Teenagers No More: Winter's Coming

NOVEMBER IS the turning of the year, the bridge between a harvest that's over and a winter that's coming.

Winter seemed very close the first Tuesday morning in November. It was cold, and rain slanted earthward in long streams. I scurried indoors, clutching a bag of thawing chicken nuggets—my fairly flop-proof contribution to the noon meal.

Leaves showered from the maples in a golden-brown deluge. They blanketed the lawn in front of the porch, spread in an even tawny carpet over the circle drive, over the grass and the top of the trampoline, and beneath the swings. Drifts of them nestled in every flower bed, and by twos or tens they scuttled like crabs moving sideways, end over end across the porch ahead of the cold gusts of wind.

Wreaths of woodsmoke curled from the chimney, and the stove in the kitchen snacked contentedly on chunks of wood. The house was warm, the teakettle purred, and for a brief space of time winter was shut out.

Mom had moved her houseplants indoors, and pots of them were grouped in corners or lined up on window sills. They snuggled together in the warmth, and if such a thing were possible I would have declared they were grinning smugly at the gale swirling just beyond the window panes.

Regina brought along a bucket of malted milk balls for us to snack on, and we did so with appreciation. There's nothing that works quite like chocolate and a wood fire to warm a cold day.

Jerelyn must have agreed. She pulled a chair close to the stove, where she ate malted milk balls, read *Shining for Jesus*, and ignored the noise ebbing around her.

• • •

Luella and Janessa crouched on the linoleum beside the woodstove, working on a floor puzzle. It had huge pieces, which they were fitting together in various ways, trying to help a large red barn with a silo and many animals emerge from the confusion.

David walked all over it in his attempt to help. The girls sat back on their heels to eye him with disfavor. "Ashley can crawl now," Janessa said. "Makayla and I taught her to do that."

"That was helpful of you," Ida Mae replied. "Do you think you could teach Steven too?"

Janessa seemed doubtful as she studied Steven, who waved his arms and kicked his feet and looked like he wanted to go places fast. "Steven is a little small," she said.

"Yes, he is," Ida Mae agreed. "He will learn by himself soon."

Corey and Wesley were concerned about Mom's little fairy garden. They came in from the porch looking worried. "It's broken," they told Mom, with identical dismayed expressions.

"Yes, I know. I left it outside on the table," Mom explained. "Then the wind blew it down and broke off two of the legs on the container. I couldn't find them anywhere."

Corey and Wesley looked at each other. "We can hunt for the little legs," they volunteered. "We could find them."

"Maybe you could," Mom said. "Crawl over the porch floor and check if they fell into a crack between the boards."

After a lengthy search in the cold wind, Corey and Wesley were ready to believe the legs were gone. They returned to the warm kitchen, where they discovered a book full of glossy pictures of Amish children. Side by side, they sat on the couch, the book open across their laps, and slowly turned the pages.

The pictures held their attention for a long time. "Here are horses and wagons," they told each other. "Here the men are baling hay. And these children are going to school." They scrutinized the pictures of children on swings, children with their pets, children playing games or skipping home from school, lunch boxes swinging.

"Look at those boys' hats." Wesley pointed.

Corey gazed at them, perhaps with recognition. "Hey, Wesley, we are Amish children too." Struck, maybe for the first time, by their similarities to the children in the book, they leaned against each other and giggled for a long time.

• • •

November means the last leaves falling, the first cold storms, and it also brings the large book sale in Dayton, which is always held the first weekend of the month. Usually a number of people from the community go, searching for both familiar titles and new ones.

Mom brought home a few boxes of potential library material, and we were glad for a chance to rummage through all the books. We offered to review the interesting titles for her library, and to buy our favorite ones for our personal libraries at home. We are such helpful daughters.

When we had discussed each title and author to our satisfaction, we stacked them back into the boxes. All winter long we'll help ourselves to new reading material from those boxes, return them to Mom with the verdict—library material or not library material—and haul a new pile along home.

Our husbands agree that sometimes we have more books than sense. But they are usually laughing when they say it, so we aren't to blame if we can't take them too seriously.

. • • •

"Makayla, guess what I saw last week at school," I said. It had been my turn to serve a hot lunch there in November, and then Laverne and I also visited both classrooms to see Alisha and Matthan at work.

When Makayla couldn't guess I said, "KellyAnn at school, sounding out new words."

It had been the special moment of my visit, watching Matthan and KellyAnn with the first-grade class at the front of the room, using the alphabet sounds they had already learned to begin reading long lists of words on the chart.

Makayla smiled. Amanda shook her head. "It's a bit mind-boggling to me to see how fast those little first-grade children learn."

"It sure is," Ida Mae agreed. "Melody is already reading words too, and it doesn't seem possible. Did they learn that fast when I was a teacher?"

"Yes, but when we were the teachers we were with them every day," Amanda pointed out. "Maybe that's why it seems so much faster now."

Maybe that is the reason. Because it is really astonishing to me too, that these three little children we sent to first grade just two months ago are now ready for their first reading books. It's enough to make my head ache.

But then, it already aches most of the time lately, so it doesn't take much to produce an extra throb or two. I'd worn my reading glasses today, causing Wesley and Makayla and Luella to give me questioning second and third glances to be sure they were seeing whom they thought they were seeing. And still I squinted to read the signature on the card I held.

"If you have on your glasses," Mom said, "why do you hold the card at a slant to look at it?"

"I need new ones, I suppose," I answered, between a sigh and a moan. "I scheduled an appointment at the vision center, but it's still two weeks away. I'm not sure I'll still be sane by then, because I just can't read much."

"Couldn't you have made an appointment earlier?" someone asked, reasonably enough.

"Of course I could have. But it came so gradually. I already had constant headaches and severe eyestrain before I realized what was wrong."

"Your eyes must be changing fast," Mom commented. "There was a time I had to go for new glasses every few years too. The eye doctor explained that between age forty and fifty your eyes, and the way they focus, can change quite a bit. Since I'm older I don't have that problem anymore."

What a relief to hear that. Not that my eyes are aging, exactly, but rather that it's normal and not the result of too much reading and writing. Surely new glasses will fix the problem.

• • •

November afternoons were the perfect time to knot the three comforters Mom had made with extra fabric pieces. All that remained to be done before they could be donated to Christian Aid Ministries was putting in the knots.

The extra leaves stayed in the long kitchen table after dinner, and we spread the blankets over it. Scissors, needles, and yarn were fetched, and chairs lined up in front of it. We were ready to start.

But first we had to thread the yarn through the eyes of the large needles, and a hard job it was. Emily tried for a while. So did I. The yarn refused to cooperate by sliding into the needle's eye.

Mom showed us how she did it. "It's really not that hard. Hold the yarn so it's hidden between your thumb and finger, and put the eye of the needle right up to the spot. Then slowly move the needle back toward it, and the yarn slides right in."

She demonstrated, and we tried it that way instead of poking the yarn at the needle. We had to make several tries, but at last it worked for us too. Threading yarn into the needles was no longer a problem. In fact, after a while I took over the job and spent my time refilling all the empty needles.

The knotting progressed faster then. A threaded needle was always ready and waiting. As the last remnant of yarn was yanked through the material and knotted into place, the needle was snipped off and handed to me, and traded for a full one.

We filled mugs with coffee (surprisingly, there were no spills), the kettle hummed on the stove, and the kitchen was warm. We knotted comforters and talked.

Mom asked if any of us had a copy of an old poem, for which she knew only the first two lines: "I loaded my camel rich and high / And headed toward the needle's eye."

None of us had ever heard of it. But it made for an interesting discussion about the real "needle's eye," the small door in the wall of ancient Jerusalem by which travelers could enter after the main gates were already closed for the night. And this was the gate Jesus used in his comparison when he said, "It is easier for a camel to go through the eye of a needle, than for a rich man to enter into the kingdom of God" (Matthew 19:24).

"But I've read that it actually was possible for a camel to go through that door," Mom said. "If it got down on its knees and dropped everything it carried on its back."

"One of the ministers talked about that in his sermon not so long ago," Ida Mae recalled. "He used it as a comparison for us too, about getting on our knees and dropping the things we carry so we can come to God."

• • •

One Tuesday we ordered some of Mom's pizza for dinner the following week. "I'm hungry for your homemade pizza," Amanda told Mom. "If I bring the cheese along, could you make some for me next week?"

"And I could bring the meat or something," Emily offered.

"There's still some pepperoni in the freezer that you'd brought along weeks ago," Mom said. "And if you want pizza, why, of course I can make some."

The rest of us decided to contribute salad fixings to the meal, and so it was that the following week we brought plastic baggies stuffed with various ingredients: grated cheese, bacon bits, diced ham, and summer sausage, plus radishes, carrots, and lettuce.

We reminded Mom of two things—we still wanted her pizza for dinner, and about an old saying whose origin has been lost in obscurity: "A son's a son till he gets a wife. But a daughter's a daughter all her life."

Today we'd just asked for a pizza. But we're not above raiding Mom's cupboards and pantry shelves if we need something and won't get to the store that week. It embarrasses our children as they grow older, but Mom doesn't seem to mind.

Mom mixed up a double batch of pizza crust, and we dodged each other's elbows as we all worked at the sink. Jerelyn washed the lettuce and carrots, and we ransacked the freezer for pepperoni, grated the radishes, tore up a head of lettuce, crumbled the homemade summer sausage, and fetched a quart jar of Mom's canned sausage from the cellar.

We ended up with a delicious-looking pizza. The salad looked delicious too.

"I dumped this baggie full of diced ham into the lettuce," Emily remarked while assembling the salad.

"But I brought that for the pizza," Amanda protested.

Emily studied the lettuce and grated veggies in the bowl. "Come to think of it, I also put the summer sausage in here."

Jerelyn came to peer over Emily's shoulder. "That was for the pizza too."

"The bacon bits are in here as well," Emily said. "Today we'll eat a three-meat salad."

The day was mild again, and the children played outside as we worked. They ran from the trampoline, down the hill to the greenhouses, and back again, swirling dry brown leaves in their wake.

They trudged uphill more slowly the last time they came, lugging plastic pots heavy with potting soil and a few straggly stems of long-dead flowers. These they placed beside carriage or bike cart, to be loaded up later, to the consternation of their moms.

They blew in the door when it was nearly dinnertime, rosy cheeked and smelling of fresh air and making enough noise for twice as many children.

Wesley and Corey had been guard dogs, guarding the trampoline. "Grr, grr, grr," they growled while scrubbing their dirty hands.

"But we were little ponies," Makayla explained as she and Janessa and Luella trotted briskly after them.

Amanda was squeezing lemons for fresh lemonade. It is a family tradition. Homemade pizza tastes so much better with freshly squeezed lemonade. She arranged thin slices to float in the clear glass pitcher before placing it on the table.

The row of thirsty children on the bench set up an immediate clamor. "I want a lemon peel," they requested in their outdoor voices, and with much banging of cups. "I want lemon slices. I want to eat the lemon peels. Please put a slice in my cup."

"There are enough lemon slices for all of you to have some," Amanda said, and began forking slices into children's cups.

"I want a flower to take home," Janessa was begging. "Please, Mom. Can I take flowers home from the greenhouse?"

"Flowers?" Amanda asked in disbelief. "Flowers now? You'd better wait until it's spring again."

"Janessa, you sound like me," I said. "I'd like to start over planting flowers again."

"Do you want to be Darla's little girl for a while?" Amanda asked Janessa. But Janessa declined the offer, flower planting or not.

It was a delicious three-meat salad. The pizza was as delicious as it looked, hot and dripping with meat and cheese and sauce. We praised it with enthusiasm.

"It must be the homemade, home-smoked sausage that adds a touch of extra flavor," Mom said.

But Janessa liked the cookies best of all. "They have docolate dips," she told Luella happily, showing Luella the large cookie she had chosen. "Big docolate dips."

• • •

Late in the month there came a November afternoon that was mild and sunny, and we seized the opportunity to tackle the yearly leaf raking that is never quite done. We just give up at last, and the final leaves drop and blow away on the winter winds.

When the dishes were put away, we donned sweaters or light jackets and made for the door. "Children, get your coats," we called. "Let's go rake leaves."

Alas, it's never quite that simple. Wesley leaped up from his play and called the alarm. "The moms are going outside to rake leaves!"

Dolls and books and toys were discarded immediately. The children clamored around, shrieking, "Run, run, get my coat, the moms are all going outside." And the few who had previously shed their shoes began to panic. "Mom! Mom, I need my shoes. Where are my shoes? I can't find my shoes!" And it was left to each mom to locate the errant shoe, which was generally hidden in the strangest place she thought to look.

At last, all properly clad and shod, we arrived at our destination—the front yard. Mom hauled four rakes from the cellar, a large plastic tub, and a sheet. We set to work with energy and determination. On the right side of the house we raked huge piles of leaves downhill, our stopping point being the cluster of lilac bushes we called Lilac Hill. The leaves were piled among the lilacs, and spread out to mulch the area around and underneath the bushes.

The piles quickly formed mammoth heaps, and Wesley and Corey pulled the empty tub uphill, where we filled it, and they ran downhill with it piled full. Leaves scattered behind them, but they managed to transfer most of their load to the center of the bushes. Here they were building Native American homes, they told us, as they hauled still more leaves downhill and dug holes in the enormous piles.

We raked until the grass on that side of the house showed green again and most of the fallen leaves were mulching the lilacs. Then we puffed back uphill, heads tipped upward to examine the amount of remaining leaves still clinging to the mostly bare branches in the webbed network high overhead.

"We got most of them," was our verdict. "The rest can blow away."

The children's fun in the leaves on Lilac Hill was over too. Luella happened to get a blackberry thorn in her hand and shed many tears. The homes in the bushes were forgotten, and the children tagged along to the second part of the lawn.

Here we employed a king-sized flat sheet. When the piles of leaves rose to monstrous proportions, we spread the sheet in front of the pile, and two or three of us transferred the pile of leaves to the sheet with our rakes. The four corners were gathered together to form a gigantic, bulging sack, which we dragged to the side of the barn. There we dropped one corner of the sheet, and the leaves poured out against the side of the barn, where they would compost all winter. We dragged the empty sheet back for another load.

The children all worked hard. Luella and Janessa became horses, "hitched" to the plastic tub with twine, and they dragged many loads of leaves to the compost pile with their tub "wagon." Corey, Wesley, and Makayla helped with the sheet as it traveled back and forth, back and forth, on countless journeys.

When the pile beside the barn was so vast as to defy repeated shakings with the sheet, the children set up residence there. They wallowed in the pile, packing it down for us, and dug holes, where they nestled like little rabbits and yelled for us to pour the leaves over them.

They played there for as long as we worked, and Jerelyn took care of the babies in the house. And we labored on for a long time, with more determination than energy by then, but intending to finish, whatever it took.

At last the leaves were conquered and the rakes hung back up. We trudged indoors for glasses of water and chairs. "We are no longer teenagers," we said to each other.

I had brought Alisha's last two dresses to cut, but I packed them away in favor of coffee and conversation. We talked, then we laughed, awakening Steven, but he forgave us with a dimpled smile.

One of Mom's friends had given her a sample of homemade salve, and the name of it was Strong Woman's Salve. We passed the can around, dipping into the contents and sniffing the pleasant aroma.

"Olive oil and beeswax," read the ingredient label. "Infused with lavender, tea tree, and orange essential oils." And underneath, in smaller letters: "Plus strength and gumption."

That produced the laughter. It was the reason we all used a small portion of the salve for hand lotion. Who of us didn't need a bit of extra strength and gumption?

"I need it today for sure," I said, rubbing some on my dry hands. "I still have to bike home and houseclean two rooms. We're getting overnight guests next week."

No doubt about it, if we could absorb some doses of strength and gumption from that salve, we all needed some just about then.

• • •

Toward the end of the month we turned our attention to Thanksgiving and the meal we were all sharing at Regina's house after church services in the morning. Nathan would be home from Alaska, the harvest season was over for another year, and Thanksgiving was marked on the calendar. It was time to thank God for family, for freedom, for food and shelter and all the abundant blessings he showers upon us daily, hourly.

Food, of course, is the main element of the Thanksgiving meal. In the weeks before Thanksgiving, our conversation centers there quite often, and on such enthralling topics as holiday turkey prices, and whether Butterball brand turkeys are better than any other brand.

"I need to copy your recipe for cranberry salad," one of us will say to Mom.

And: "If a recipe asks for heavy cream, is that the same as the whipping cream you buy in the store?"

Or: "I'm hungry for pimento dip with crackers, Mom. Do you still have some?"

To which Mom would reply, "Yes, I have lots of canned pimento mix in jars in the cellar. And plenty of cream cheese in the fridge. I'll make some."

The seasons keep swinging, and the years keep passing, and time is like a relentless tide that never hurries, never waits, never stops. It takes us all along, whether we notice or not, whether we like it or not.

As everything changes in one way or another, we continue to cherish family and make it our highest priority. After all, other people are the only thing on earth that you can take along to heaven. Where better, then, to invest your time and your life, than in other people? And especially those you encounter most often.

There is a timelessness in love—love for God first, then love for those around us. And of that love, the ties of a family legacy are the most precious.

It's easy to remember that during the good times, the times of thanksgiving and days of laughter. It's harder to keep that firmly fixed in one's heart when the hard times come, the storms, the tests. But why thank God only for good things, sunshine, happiness, laughter?

I'm still learning to say thank you as well for the difficulties, the rain, the times of tears. But those times are the ones that bring growth, make us stronger, send roots deeper into faith, and trust in God's ultimate plan.

Thanksgiving is not just a day that arrives on the calendar once a year and gives us a chance to get together and celebrate with cranberry relish and turkey and stuffing and desserts. It's a heart condition for those who love God and believe in his divine love and salvation and guidance.

• • •

*"Giving thanks always for all things unto God and the
Father in the name of our Lord Jesus Christ."*

EPHESIANS 5:20

DECEMBER

Giddyup:
Christmas, plus Year's End
Comes Careening

Who loves the rain and loves his home,
and looks on life with quiet eyes,
him will I follow through the storm,
and at his hearth-fire keep me warm.

—FRANCES SHAW, "WHO LOVES THE RAIN"[3]

IN DECEMBER, Tuesdays often take a little more effort. More layers of coats and jackets and gloves and socks and boots. More cold weather, sometimes complete with snow and ice, when venturing outdoors.

But when Monday's work is done and Tuesday morning rolls around again, we bundle up with many clothes, some grunting and groaning, and head out the door. Then the fresh air and delicious cold invigorate and refresh, from nose to doubting toes, and it's not so bad to be outside after all.

It was snowing when I arrived at Mom's, the first snow of the winter. The ground had slowly turned white, and when I walked to the porch the flat rocks of the front walk were covered.

Corey and Wesley were playing in front of the porch. They were taking advantage of that first fluffy inch, rolling in it and jumping around like puppies. They looked up and saw me. "We're making snow angels," Wesley said, pointing to the shapes in the snow behind them.

"Our snow angels," Corey agreed, showing me.

Oh. Not puppies after all. I admired the dents in the snow. "Those are nice snow angels," I said, for on closer inspection I could see the wings and heads and skirts. "Very pretty angels."

Inside, the house was warm and noisy and cluttered with all our things. Behind the house an engine chugged as Dad fed chunks of venison into the grinder. Mom urged us to fill plastic bags with the ground meat to take home. "I don't need that much venison anymore," she insisted.

I was only too happy to help myself. "I'm almost out of ground beef," I told Ida Mae as we filled bags and closed them with twist ties. "Like all food at our house these days, it just vanishes."

"We had some fresh venison earlier," Ida Mae said. "That's all gone already too. Luella wasn't impressed about the thought of venison, though. We took to calling it speed beef, and then she decided it tasted fine after all."

I could sympathize a little with Luella. I was never fond of venison, or ground beef either, for that matter. But when you have a family to cook for you learn the value of meat in a hurry.

Since there was so much fresh meat available we decided to make mock ham balls for dinner. The recipe asked for one pound of ground beef, but we prepared two batches. To two pounds of ground venison we added crushed cracker crumbs, salt, eggs, and pepper. I fastened the hand-cranked grinder to the table, and Mom handed me a pack of hot dogs. Wesley came running. "I want to help grind the hot dogs," he cried.

"Here you go." I handed him one of the hot dogs and showed him in which direction to crank the handle. He fed the hot dog into the mouth of the grinder and cranked fast. In no time at all we had a pile of ground-up hot dogs to add to the venison. Mom mixed everything together and formed the mixture into little balls to line up in rows in the pan. Emily mixed the sauce.

MOCK HAM BALLS

    1 pound ground venison (or ground beef)
    ½ pound hot dogs, ground
    1 cup crushed cracker crumbs
    1 egg
    1 teaspoon salt
    ½ teaspoon pepper

Mix together all ingredients and form into small meatballs. Place in rows in baking dish.

Glaze

    ¾ cup brown sugar
    ½ cup water
    ½ teaspoon vinegar

Mix and pour over meatballs. Bake at 350°F for 1 hour.

• • •

I had delayed cutting out more dresses to sew for Alisha as long as I possibly could. It had to be done now. I pulled out the bag holding the pattern and both pieces of fabric, and searched through Mom's sewing machine drawer for scissors and a tape measure.

One piece of fabric was rose colored, the second lavender. Makayla came to watch. "May I have the scraps of material?" she asked.

"Of course you may." I shook open the first piece. "As soon as I have some for you. But I haven't even started yet."

"I could cut them for you," Makayla offered. She pretended her fingers were a pair of scissors and zoomed along imaginary lines. "Cut, cut, cut. Now I've done Alisha's dresses."

"You forgot to use the pattern," I said, holding it up. Makayla giggled. Then she stood at the table, waiting for the first scraps.

She waited a long time. Wesley, Janessa, and Luella came to wait with her, and still there were no fabric pieces coming their way. I labored along straight lines, measuring and cutting out pieces for skirt and apron. They gave up and went to play again.

At last I was cutting along slanting lines, slicing off strangely shaped pieces. When I was done I gathered up the scraps and went to find the children.

They had set up a school in the middle room, using small chairs, plus the couch as a desk, for multiple "students." Then they raided the library for picture books and sat at their "desk," turning the pages of the books. Except for the times they wanted to trade books, which was every half minute. So it was that their school was more about jumping up and exchanging books than about actually sitting down and studying.

Regina brought them papers and pens. "Now you can practice your writing too," she told them. Then she returned to her
comforter patches. She was cutting them from various shades
of brown and black fabric, patterned and solid colored.

I picked up the pattern for the latest blanket she was making.
It was called Spice and resembled the Log Cabin pattern. "I am
so glad I don't have to do that for fun," I said.

Ashley crawled out from under the table and clutched at
Regina's dress. Regina picked her up and Ashley snuggled into
her arms. She had found her mom, she thought.

We laughed quietly to ourselves and wondered how long it
would be before she discovered she had found the wrong mom
to cuddle her. Minutes passed. Ashley was sleepy and content.
Then she heard Amanda talking behind her. She sat up and re-
garded Regina with an incredulous scrutiny. "This is not my
mom?" she seemed to be saying.

She turned around and studied Amanda. Then, with a sheepish little smile, she squirmed toward her. Ashley had found her
real mom after all.

• • •

There were Marjolein Bastin calendars lying on top of Mom's
sewing machine, paintings by her favorite artist for each month
of the new year. And Amanda brought her a new one.

"I happened to see this one and decided it was one of her
prettiest paintings yet," Amanda explained.

How could it be that we were thinking about changing calendars already? Didn't the year just start, and already we were
careening to the end? Each year goes faster than the one before.
They spin circles like the children were doing now—running

circles through the rooms, some of them wearing jump ropes for harnesses, and others flapping the ends of the ropes for reins and calling, "Giddyup! Faster, faster."

The years go fast too. And faster and faster the minutes gallop away.

• • •

Regina stood at the sink with a bowl of soft pretzel dough. David stood at her skirts, demanding his share of attention. "Does anyone want to roll and twist the pretzels?" Regina asked. "Or hold David for me while I do it?"

I offered to hold David. "You can be my little baby for a while," I told him as we settled into a rocking chair. "We'll look at the pictures in this magazine." I picked up the most recent issue of *Our Iowa* lying on the end table.

David cooperated nicely. We rocked and studied the winter pictures. Regina filled trays with soft pretzels.

Mom turned the gas oven dial to 450 to preheat the oven. Nothing happened. She opened the kitchen drawer and searched for a long-handled lighter. "Maybe if I hold this to the pilot light the oven burners will light. But what if I blow up the oven instead?"

Again nothing happened. The pilot light continued its unconcerned flickering. The oven didn't blow up, but neither did it light.

"Well, what could be wrong?" Mom asked, getting down on her knees and peering into the nether regions of the oven. Emily offered to give it a try with the lighter. David and I went to give our advice and suggestions. The oven still sulked, refusing to either light or blow up.

"Let me add some more wood to the stove in the kitchen," Mom said at last. "We'll bake the pretzels in there."

"Can you get the oven on the woodstove as hot as four fifty?" Regina asked.

"Probably not in such a short time," Mom answered, piling some more chunks of firewood into the stove all the same. "The pretzels will just have to bake at a lower temperature today."

The soft pretzels baked slowly, but they baked. They were a little flat when we took them out and buttered them, but they tasted fine. We smothered them in cheese sauce and enjoyed them anyhow.

We discussed recipes, and various Christmas doings at school, and the amazing results of Liquid Gold furniture polish when used to clean. Corey and Wesley discussed the beaver dams they had created on their plates, and all the variations of beavers and their bites, as demonstrated on their food.

• • •

In one way or another, most of the month is geared toward Christmas. Christmas cards and letters, Christmas cookies and treats of all shapes and sizes and colors, Christmas carol singings and programs at school.

Somehow it seems fitting to wrap up the old year with the spirit of Christmas as a celebration of the birth of Jesus, and to take the memory of that happy occasion over two thousand years ago along into the new year. Not the commercialization of holidays minus Christ, perhaps, but more a joyous acknowledgment of the baby who was born once so that we could be born again into his kingdom.

For the birth of the baby who was King is only the beginning. The manger is the prelude to the cross, just as

Bethlehem always leads to Golgotha on Good Friday. For the divine baby of the virgin birth, who slept in the feed trough of an ox or donkey, Christmas was—and still is for us—only the beginning. The manger is the prelude to the cross, just as the cross is the way into the heavenly kingdom that stands forever. And that's Christmas to me—the hidden manger in the lonely Bethlehem hills, the torturous cross as punishment for the Man who had never sinned, and the glorious resurrection morning when all those who live for and die with Christ will see his forever kingdom. Which is why he was born in the first place, and why he said to us, "Ye must be born again" (John 3:7).

• • •

The line of Christmas cards on the wall behind the table in the kitchen lengthened weekly. It was directly behind the bench where the children sat to eat dinner, and so it was that Corey, Wesley, Makayla, and Janessa finished the last bites on their plates while seated backward. They were examining the pictures on each card and talking to each other.

"Christmas is Jesus' birthday," remarked Wesley to Corey as they studied a manger scene.

Corey nodded seriously. "Yes, it is."

"Christmas is when Jesus was born," Makayla agreed. "But then he grew up and died."

"It was the bad men that killed him," Wesley said. "They put him on a cross."

"And he died," Janessa said sadly.

"But he didn't stay died," Makayla reminded her, sounding awed. "He's alive again."

Wesley nodded with five-year-old wisdom. "And that's really true."

"It's as true as true," Makayla said, still looking awed.

• • •

Christmas is a season of celebration and happiness and time spent with family. Perhaps we celebrate the day in a more low-key fashion than many people, but we celebrate it in our own way, and with joy remember the baby from Bethlehem, who came to die so we could live.

He came with the first Christmas gift of his own for all people everywhere who surrender to the message he brought from God, his Father. His gift came to us when he died so that we could be born again as new people with new hearts, Christ-centered. The way each of us lives shows whether we've rejected or accepted his Christmas gift.

And that's the spirit of holy joy to take along into the new year. When the last package is opened, the last cookie and candy consumed, the last wrapping paper discarded, Christmas really has only just begun.

• • •

Mom put a plate filled with her Christmas cookies on the table: chocolate crinkles, walnut frosties, peanut dreams, cherry winks. I saved mine to have with coffee later that afternoon.

WALNUT FROSTIES

1 cup margarine or butter

2 cups brown sugar

2 eggs, beaten

2 teaspoons vanilla

4 cups all-purpose flour

1 teaspoon baking soda

½ teaspoon salt

In a large bowl, combine all ingredients; blend well, then shape into 1-inch balls. Place on cookie sheets and make a depression in center, using the handle of a butter knife dipped in flour so it does not stick to dough. Prepare topping.

Walnut topping

2 cups ground walnuts

¾ cup brown sugar

½ cup sour cream

Combine and mix well. Spoon 1 teaspoon walnut topping onto center of each cookie. Bake at 350°F until delicately browned.

We put the last dishes away, on that last Tuesday of the year, and took down mugs for coffee and cappuccino. The teakettle steamed ready, the cookie platter was full again, and we sat around the table once more, talking, eating, busy with handwork.

Regina crocheted on her latest afghan, a cream-colored creation with variegated lines of pink, jade, and chocolate yarn.

Ida Mae worked on baby booties. Emily and Amanda had their pencil boxes, as usual stuffed with stamped pictures and Prisma colored pencils.

And I—I was so tired of writing, mostly because my new glasses made my eyes hurt more, not less—that I colored one of Amanda's pictures for her.

It was a picture of roses. I colored the flowers red and the leaves green. Not much to it, I thought.

But Amanda gaped at me from one side. "Can you believe this? She's coloring a picture," she exclaimed to Emily, who was leaning over her own picture and staring at me from the other side.

"No, I can't believe this," Emily replied. "We'll turn her into a card-stamper yet."

I pretended not to know what the fuss was all about. I was just coloring one picture, after all. It wasn't like I was going to make an entire card.

Makayla colored violets on one side of me. Luella colored too, and an interesting picture emerged, with pink trees, brown clouds, a blue horse, and orange leaves.

Janessa came to help. Not much more was happening. I drank my coffee and colored another picture.

• • •

The afternoon drifted away in this languorous manner. Regina told us about David's latest job, which had been painting the floor with an entire bottle of correction fluid while she worked.

"And you can't believe how hard it was to scrub that off the linoleum," she said.

Mom told us about the beads and tiny toy animals she had discovered in her potted plants and vines all week long after last

Tuesday. Beads dangled beside the green vines, and plastic yellow duckies and small white Dalmatians peeped from beneath the leaves.

"We were having a zoo," Corey, Wesley, and Makayla explained.

"I felt a little as if I were having a treasure hunt all week," Mom said.

The children were each allowed to choose two books from the library to take home, but before tucking their selections away into bags, they perched in a long line on the couch and gazed at the pictures. They talked to each other and found sources for lengthy discussions on the bright pages. They were absorbed in their books, and all was peaceful, for that moment.

Mom had a list of books from a store called Loreen's Used Books, and discovered a title for a friend, who for years had been seeking a copy of *White Robin*, by British author Miss Read, published perhaps half a century ago.

"We'll buy it and give it to her for a gift," Mom and I decided together. "It will be fun to surprise her."

This was our final gathering for the year, around Mom's kitchen table, where we shed for a little while all the cares and responsibilities of adulthood and pretended for a few hours to be girls again. Not quite as carefree as we used to be, maybe, for these days we talk about our children and homemaking and all the various duties of school and church and home. We probably discuss bills and taxes at least as often as our weight, and our plans and goals for the future are a great deal more down-to-earth and yet more centered in God's plan for our lives than they used to be.

But sisters we are, and always will be, and Tuesdays with Mom are part of the fabric from which our adult lives are woven. Each week we come, through cold and heat and rain and snow, and keep warm for a time at the hearth-fires of our old home. Then, renewed, refreshed, restored, we leave to meet head-on the life we've been given.

The children giggled together over their books. Through the window above the couch we watched a bluebird in a hanging basket on the porch, eating the bittersweet berries on the vines Mom had looped there.

The coffee cooled, the cookie tray emptied. We colored and crocheted and talked. A year of Tuesdays had drifted to an end. But another one was just beginning.

• • •

"For he is our peace."

EPHESIANS 2:14

A Day in the Life
of the Author

TUESDAY, FEBRUARY 6, 2018

Good morning.

5:00 a.m. Some of my days begin at five in the morning and some of them at six. This one starts at five when I get up to make Cody's breakfast. On the days that he works at the pallet shop in an Amish community about thirty miles from here, the alarm clock wakes us an hour earlier than usual.

Cody finishes packing his lunch while I scramble eggs and bring a jar of blackberry juice up from the basement. I pack Matthan's lunch in between various morning duties in the kitchen, then I have my breakfast too, with coffee and a brief dive between the covers of a book. This morning I'm reading *The Blessings of Brokenness* by Charles Stanley.

Laverne's morning work consists of feeding the animals in the barn and feeding two furnaces as well. The one in the basement warms the house, and another keeps the furniture shop warm. Together they consume great heaps of firewood during this unusually cold winter.

6:00 a.m. The van driver who hauls the pallet shop workers is right on time, and Cody is the first to leave this morning. He's sixteen and works in the shop here at home on other days. In less than two months his summer jobs will begin—working on a produce farm and at the produce auction.

After Cody is off to work it's time to wake Alisha and Matthan and help them get ready for school. Alisha is fourteen and in her last term, grade eight, at Fairview School.

Matthan is six. He trots off to first grade matter-of-factly, as he does most things; he has learned to read, write, and do math, also matter-of-factly. I, on the other hand, am astonished all over again by the sponge-like qualities of these little minds. They absorb and remember such vast stacks of knowledge every day.

After they've had breakfast, Alisha needs help to put up her hair and Matthan needs help with his clothes. There are also pets to care for. Alisha's cats number seven, and they are lined up on the porch waiting for their morning rations of milk and cat food. Matthan's four parakeets need fresh water.

7:30 a.m. I'm in the last stages of getting schoolchildren out the door. It's twenty-four degrees. That feels almost balmy compared to temperatures we had last month, but it's still cold enough to require multiple layers of clothes.

"Spring will certainly be welcome this year," I say as I help Matthan wrestle his insulated snow pants over his other pants for the two-and-a-half-mile bike ride to school.

Matthan isn't thinking about spring. He's thinking—of all things—about octopuses.

"I don't like those octopuses," he says. "They are my enemies. If it wasn't for the suction cups on the ends of their legs, they wouldn't be so bad. I'm never going near where octopuses are, but if I were fishing in the ocean and caught one, do you know what I would do? I would cut my line."

At last he's wearing an outer layer of thick clothes, including an extra item or two to keep *me* warm.

7:40 a.m. We go to the basement for their bikes. "See you," I call after them as they wheel out the door and to the lane. "Have a good day."

Suddenly it's quiet. I fill a basket with yesterday's clean laundry still waiting to be folded, and go upstairs again.

8:15 a.m. After helping Laverne unload some heavy cabinets, I'm ready for my weekly dose of sisters at Mom's house, with coffee, conversation, laughter, and stories. I rush around doing some last-minute things, collect the food I've prepared, and start off.

The floors aren't swept and the laundry isn't folded, but I'm fairly certain it'll all be waiting for me when I return after another ordinary Tuesday at Mom's house.

3:15 p.m. Home again. So are Alisha and Matthan. And just as I thought, the floor still isn't swept and the laundry still needs to be put away. I work at that, water the houseplants, and listen to tales about the children's day at school. Before I know it, it's time to start supper preparations.

5:30 p.m. Cody arrives home from his day at the pallet shop.

6:00 p.m. Suppertime. It's much later tonight, for Laverne is busy with a customer, but at last he comes to the house. The children have already eaten, and I'm reading letters in *Die Botschaft*, an Amish and Old Order Mennonite newspaper that Mom shares with me.

Since supper was late, devotions are late too. We're reading in the book of Mark, chapter 8, tonight. Then Laverne goes to finish shop work, Alisha does the dishes, and Cody reads a book. I listen to Alisha and Matthan studying the poems they'll recite at the program at school later this month, and tidy up the kitchen.

8:00 p.m. I've helped Matthan get into his pajamas, read a Bible story and two other stories for him, and tucked him into bed. He's tired and is soon sound asleep. Morning, and another school day, will come soon enough.

Alisha spends the next hour reading or making stamped-art cards. Cody is tired and goes to bed early.

I would have some journaling to do, or books to read, but my eyes keep wanting to close. Five in the morning is starting to seem like a long time ago.

9:30 p.m. Laverne finishes up the barn chores, including milking the cow, and brings the milk to the house. My last job of the day is straining the milk into plastic jugs, putting it in the fridge, and washing the pail with hot water.

It's been an ordinary day—blessedly ordinary, and filled with family and work, faith and living. May tomorrow be the same.

"The grass withereth, the flower thereof falleth away: But the word of the Lord endureth forever" (1 Peter 1:24-25).

FAQ *about Old Order Mennonites:* The Author Answers

Author Darla Weaver answers some frequently asked questions about Old Order Mennonite life, faith, and culture.

What is it like to be a Mennonite?

In some ways it's really not so different from being anyone else. We have one life to live; we work to make a living, take care of our families, make time for the things we enjoy, eat, sleep, pay our bills and taxes. Some days are better than others, as for anyone else.

In other ways it's vastly different from the culture around us. Partly in the conservative way we live; perhaps even more in the way we look at life.

The most important goals for most of us are faith in God and in his Son, who died on the cross for sinners; growing in a closer walk with him; learning to love, serve, and obey his commandments. These beliefs help shape our lives as we grow older.

Old Order Mennonite life is family-oriented. It centers on our church, our families, our schools and neighborhoods. It has been said, "Destroy the home and you destroy the nation," which has been proven true in various eras of history. God's plan for one husband and one wife, working together to care for their children, is a most important foundation for our lifestyle.

But of course, we are far from perfect. Although the majority of us strive to live lives that demonstrate a faith and love and steadfastness rooted deep in God and his Word—the Bible—we make plenty of mistakes too. Stumbling and falling and getting up to try again, praying that God will help us do better tomorrow, is a part of life too.

Do Old Order Mennonites believe in the new birth?

Of course. We believe the Bible truth: "Except a man be born again, he cannot see the kingdom of God" (John 3:3).

It is when one believes that Jesus Christ is the Son of God that God's Spirit comes into one's heart. It is by repenting of and turning away from our sins that they can be forgiven. It is by faith in God's power, and asking in prayer, that helps us break away from sin's strongholds. And it is because of that new birth that we desire to live a life that God can bless and sanctify.

But those who grow up in Christian homes may not always be able to pinpoint a certain day or year when their new birth occurred. To ask "When were you born again?" is a little like asking "When did you grow up?" Sometimes there is a specific date to remember. Just as often there isn't, because we grew so gradually into the awareness of our need for a personal Savior.

Was there ever a time I didn't know and believe that Jesus Christ is the Son of God who came to die for my sins? If so, I can't remember it. I did have to come to the place where I was willing to accept that for myself, acknowledge all the sin in my life, and turn to God for help and forgiveness. That day came, gradually. And when I asked Christ into my heart to be Ruler there, it led to more years of growing up, and into what it means to be one of his disciples.

When I was born physically I still had much to learn. When I was born again spiritually I had just as much to learn about living a Christ-centered life. I'm still learning about it. I imagine I'll be learning more for as long as I live.

What are your church services like?

Church services last around two to two and a half hours and are in the Pennsylvania Dutch dialect, although the Bible reading is done in German. The service begins with everyone singing together. One of the ministers then has a short sermon, which is followed by silent prayer. Then a second minister explains a chapter from the New Testament, or part of a chapter that he had selected and studied previously. Services are closed with an audible prayer, more singing, and the benediction.

It's a special time of singing, praying, and worshiping God together with our congregation, and is full of encouragement and inspiration.

Why are your businesses closed on Sunday?

"Remember the sabbath day, to keep it holy. Six days shalt thou labour, and do all thy work" (Exodus 20:8-9).

When Sunday comes around, those of us who own businesses do close them, and most of our work is put aside. Sunday is kept as a day to go to church to worship God, and then spend it socializing with family and friends. It is a day to get together for meals, visit families who have a new baby, or just relax at home.

Sometimes when it's warm we go fishing or hiking at nearby state parks or in our own woods, go on picnics, or visit the neighbors. In the evening the youth group gathers at one of their homes to play volleyball, sing, and eat.

Sunday is set aside for worship, rest, and family time. It's refreshing, both spiritually and physically, to have one day each week reserved for that. Work almost always waits. Worshiping God is first priority. And then, being with family.

What do your youth do?

Most of the young people are part of a structured youth group that gathers each Sunday evening in one of their homes. If it's warm they play volleyball, before singing hymns. A snack is served, unless everyone is invited for supper, and then an entire meal is served. This can be quite an undertaking for the hostess, depending on the size of the group.

Sunday evening gatherings are a regular thing. There are sometimes "work bees" during the week when they get together to help someone who needs it. They might go to sing at a nursing home, go skating in winter or fishing in summer, or do other upbuilding activities.

Most of the young people are a part of this group and are dedicated to serving God. But the upper teen years can be hard whether or not you're Mennonite, and there are always some who drift away and choose not to live as part of our culture.

What are your private schools like?

Parochial schools are a vital part of our neighborhoods. Three men serve as the school board for each one, and they are in charge of hiring teachers and also handle the financial part of running a school, the upkeep of the building, and any other need that comes up. They serve three-year terms and are up for one reelection at the regular yearly community meeting where all directors and trustees for various things are selected.

Most schoolhouses have two classrooms and two teachers, and the number of children attending each one varies greatly. Parents pay a yearly tuition, which covers the teachers' pay, books, other supplies, and building repairs.

Most children start first grade as soon as the term begins in September after their sixth birthday. They graduate after completing eighth grade.

Each school day starts with a Bible story, reciting the Lord's Prayer together, and singing. Lessons include, but are not limited to, reading, writing, math, spelling, English, vocabulary, history, geography, some science, and nature study. Curriculum varies a little from school to school and from one area to the next, but these are the basics.

Religion is not taught as a subject. Rather, faith in God, and Christian living as based on the Bible, is woven into almost every textbook and lesson. It's a way of life for us and can't be separated into a single subject.

ACKNOWLEDGMENTS

The idea for this book was born when Melodie Davis, editor at Herald Press, asked me, "Would you be willing to write about a year of the Tuesdays you spend with your sisters at your Mom's home?" (I suspect, that as a good editor, she knew I couldn't possibly decline when I was asked if I wanted to write another book.)

That was the beginning. I'm certainly grateful to my sisters and to Mom for allowing this idea to proceed with good humor, much graciousness, and lots of laughter. Plus a few infrequent shrieks of "Don't you *dare* write that!" I gratefully acknowledge each of you.

And then there are friends who become sisters of the heart, and I have many who inspire me—too many to name here. I'll mention three who were especially encouraging while I worked on this manuscript.

Vicky Schilling, I've never met you—you're an entire continent and culture and generation removed from me and mine— but you are a soul sister indeed. You inspired me when I thought I couldn't write another word. "I can't wait to read your 'sisters' book," you wrote, often enough that I really believed you.

Esther Martin, a friend who's not quite a sister because we happen to be born cousins instead. Thanks, Esther, for your loyal encouragement, and for being excited with me about each new book.

And Doris Brubaker, your card remains in a prominent spot on the top of my desk. I've read your words so often—"May

God guide your writing ministry"—that the card is starting to look worn. You never guessed when you wrote them how much they would mean to me.

The editors and staff at Herald Press also deserve my gratitude—they work almost as hard as I do before a book finally emerges from the first scrawls and paragraphs. Thank you, Melodie, Valerie, Sara, plus LeAnn from the marketing team.

And always, always, a special thank you to Laverne, who not only supports my writing but encourages it, and to our children, Cody, Alisha, and Matthan. You are familiar with all the hazards that go with having a wife and mother who writes—yet you continue to love me anyway. This book comes with my love and thanks.

NOTES

1   Laura Ingalls Wilder, "A Bouquet of Wild Flowers," *Missouri Ruralist*, July 20, 1917, 13.

2   Gloria Gaither, Peggy Benson, Sue Buchanan, and Joy McKenzie, *Friends through Thick and Thin* (Grand Rapids, MI: Zondervan, 1999), 142.

3   Francis Shaw, "Who Loves the Rain," in *Home Sweet Home* (Franklin, TN: Ideals Publications, 2005), 64.

Read all the books in the Plainspoken series from Herald Press

Chasing the Amish Dream: *My Life as a Young Amish Bachelor*
Loren Beachy

Gathering of Sisters: *A Year with My Old Order Mennonite Family*
Darla Weaver

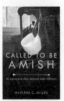

Called to Be Amish: *My Journey from Head Majorette to the Old Order*
Marlene C. Miller

FORTHCOMING FROM HERALD PRESS

The Pie Lady: *A Mennonite Cook, Her Friends, and Classic Stories from Their Kitchens*
Greta Isaac (2019)

Hutterite Diaries: *Life in my Prairie Community*
Linda Maendel

ALSO OF INTEREST: PLAINSPOKEN DEVOTIONALS

Simple Pleasures: *Stories from My Life as an Amish Mother*
Marianne Jantzi

Prayers for a Simpler Life: *Meditations from the Heart of a Mennonite Mother*
Faith Sommers

Anything but Simple: *My Life as a Mennonite*
Lucinda J. Miller

Water My Soul: *Ninety Meditations from an Old Order Mennonite*
Darla Weaver

HERALD PRESS
WWW.HERALDPRESS.COM

THE AUTHOR

Darla Weaver is a homemaker, gardener, writer, and Old Order Mennonite living in the hills of southern Ohio. She is the author of *Water My Soul* and *Many Lighted Windows* and has written for *Family Life*, *Ladies' Journal*, *Young Companion*, and other magazines for Amish and Old Order Mennonite groups. Before her three children were born she also taught school. Her hobbies are gardening and writing.

920
WEA

Weaver, Darla.

Gathering of
sisters.

$14.99

DATE			
MAY 08 2019			